TRAINING THE HIGH FLYERS

Below: The Shorts Tucano is a new generation high-performance turboprop basic trainer which combines high performance with cost effectiveness in all aspects of operation.

TRAINING THE HIGH FLYERS

Tim Laming

163

ARMS AND ARMOUR

Arms and Armour Press
A CASSELL IMPRINT
Villiers House, 41-47 Strand, London WC2N 5JE.

Distributed in the USA by Sterling Publishing Co. Inc.,
387 Park Avenue South, New York, NY 10016-8810.

Distributed in Australia by Capricorn Link (Australia)
Pty. Ltd, P.O. Box 665, Lane Cove, New South Wales
2066.

British Library Cataloguing-in-Publication Data: a
catalogue record for this book is available from the
British Library

ISBN 1-85409-154-9

Designed and edited by DAG Publications Ltd.
Designed by David Gibbons; edited by Michael
Boxall; layout by Anthony A. Evans; typeset by Ronset
Typesetters, Darwen, Lancashire; camerawork by M&E
Reproductions, North Fambridge, Essex;
Printed in Singapore by Craft Print Pte, Ltd.

Contents

Introduction

THE COLD WAR IS OVER, but peace has not prevailed, as many had expected. Despite the sweeping political changes that have effectively destroyed what was the Warsaw Pact, the world is still a violent place. The 1991 Gulf War graphically demonstrated how the post-Cold War peace can quickly be shattered in the most bloody fashion. While the politicians attempt to make sense of the constantly changing world situation, their military forces are in turmoil, and if there is an ever-growing expectation of a 'Peace Dividend' in terms of defence cuts that are now possible, thanks to the reduction of the military threat from what was the Soviet Union, there is also a great concern to preserve a credible defence strategy across NATO. Nobody can predict the political status of the world even just a year from now and, as always, it is a foolish nation that is not prepared to defend itself no matter how unlikely an armed conflict may seem.

Consequently there is clearly a continued requirement for capable defences, and as a consequence the military air arms throughout the world continue to train young men, and increasingly larger numbers of women, to fly and fight. Teaching the skills of military flying takes time and money, and a great deal of work. It is an exacting profession and only the very best succeed. It is fair to say that almost anyone can be taught to fly a modern military trainer aircraft, but for some it takes longer than others. Naturally there is only a finite amount of time and money that can be spent on each student, so today's military air arms tend to select as well as teach.

In *Training the High Flyers* I have attempted to take a broad look at the world of military flying training. I have compiled a directory of the training aircraft currently operated by the world's air forces which serves to demonstrate the huge variety of aircraft types used to teach the basics of flying and aerial warfare. Although the aircraft may vary, the ways in which students are taught to fly and fight are very similar everywhere, and while it would be difficult (and pointless) to describe individual nations' military flying training systems, it does make sense to look in more detail at what is probably the best and certainly the most widely respected one — the Royal Air Force's basic and advanced flying training syllabus. Naturally it would be impossible to trace every step of a long and detailed syllabus, but I hope that the following pages will illustrate a little of what it takes to become a military pilot in the nineties.

Below: Two Hawks climbing away over RAF Valley.

The Training

Below: Tucano on the flightline at RAF Scampton, home of the Central Flying School where the RAF teaches its instructors how to teach. In the distance is the most famous CFS squadron, the Red Arrows.

BEFORE ANY APPLICANT can be trained to become a Royal Air Force pilot he must first become a Royal Air Force Officer. Initial selection is made at the RAF OASC (Officer and Aircrew Selection Centre) at Cranwell in Lincolnshire, where the young men and women are subjected to a series of demanding tests in the form of academic and physical exercises. They are tested, monitored, interviewed, examined and questioned in minute detail. Certainly, OASC is a challenge and many applicants are rejected. Although the RAF does look for an inherent capability to fly an aircraft (testing for good hand-to-eye co-ordination in particular), other attributes are equally important, not least the right kind of character to become an officer. Flying combat aircraft is only one part of a regular RAF career, and being able to fly is just not enough.

The lucky individuals who are accepted then move to another part of RAF Cranwell, the DIOT (Department of Initial Officer Training), to undertake eighteen weeks of rigorous instruction, during which the student is taught to become an effective officer in the RAF. Although writing and other communication capabilities are emphasized, the DIOT course is intended to be much more — a broader teaching of a variety of skills, ranging from ways in which to survive for days in remote parts of the countryside, through ceremonial drill and hand arms, to the relatively simple ways to conduct oneself at a social function. A great deal is crammed into the course, and while a limitless budget and an open-ended

Left: The Royal Air Force has been in the jet training business for a long time. The Meteor (rear) and Vampire (front) were the first jet trainers to serve with the RAF until deliveries of the Jet Provost and Gnat were made.

Right: The faithful 'Chippie', on short final approach to RAF Swinderby. The landing gear is fixed in the extended position and, unlike every other RAF type, the Chipmunk is a 'tail-dragger'.

Right: Just a few feet to go, as the student lets his Chipmunk settle on to Swinderby's runway. The black markings on the wings close to the fuselage are non-slip walkways, affording access to the cockpit.

timescale would allow the instructors to produce even more capable graduates, the RAF is happy that DIOT achieves an impressive result in the time available. The students often arrive at DIOT thinking that the course is little more than a formality, but it is, in fact, much more demanding than many expect, and 'automatic graduation' is by no means certain. Students can be withdrawn if they do not measure-up to the Royal Air Force's standards, and many would-be pilots find that their RAF careers end at this early stage, before even seeing an aircraft.

Those that do successfully complete the DIOT course are finally considered ready to begin flying training. Basic flying instruction is conducted at two airfields: Linton-on-Ouse in Yorkshire, and Cranwell. Students arrive at these units from three different backgrounds. Some will have been posted to the EFTS (Elementary Flying Training School), having had no previous flying experience. They will be taught to fly the venerable piston-engined de Havilland Chipmunk during approximately 64 hours of flying instruction. The role of the EFTS is to give students a very simple grasp of flying techniques, and to allow the RAF to 'weed-out' people who are clearly unable either to absorb instruction or handle an aircraft. It makes sound financial sense to identify those who are unlikely to succeed at a very early and relatively inexpensive stage, but the EFTS does teach as well as select, and the student who moves on from the EFTS to either Cranwell or

Linton stands a very good chance of being able to handle the Tucano.

Many other students will already have significant flying experience, having flown up to 95 hours on the BAe Bulldog trainer during university and college education, at one of sixteen UAS's (University Air Squadrons) scattered around the United Kingdom. These graduates transfer directly to either 1FTS at Linton or 3FTS at Cranwell, following the DIOT course. The third category of student is someone with a minimum of thirty hours' civilian flying experience, rather less than that required to obtain a PPL (Private Pilot's Licence), but sufficient to make routeing through the EFTS unnecessary. Consequently the new arrivals at 1FTS and 3FTS have widely varying levels of experience, ranging from nearly 100 hours to virtually none.

The Royal Air Force divides its aircraft into three categories: Fast Jet, Multi-engine and Helicopter. Naturally, the fundamentals of operating all three types of aircraft are much the same, and so the new students arriving at 1FTS and 3FTS begin by working to a common course, the Basic Phase. After this initial training the RAF 'streams' the students into one of the three categories, depending upon the student's ability, aptitude and preferences. They are then given further flying instruction on Lead-In courses appropriate to each of the three types of aircraft. However, because RAF requirements for qualified pilots in each category change from time to time, students

Above left: Gear retracting, the Hawk lifts gently from Valley's runway.

Left: The large under-fuselage airbrakes are evident as two Hawks slow down before making final approach back to RAF Valley.

Above: Unique in the RAF inventory, the Chipmunk features tailwheel undercarriage.

are not always permitted to choose which type of aircraft they want to fly, and the RAF sometimes restricts FTS training to just the fast jet role, anticipating that the limited numbers of helicopter and multi-engine pilots required will be selected from students who do not successfully complete the advanced fast jet course.

The Basic Flying Training (BFT) syllabus is planned upon the assumption that much of the preparation for each sortie is carried out by the student. There are eight basic elements to the system:

■ **Ground School.** Throughout the RAF pilot's flying career time is regularly spent in ground schools. Whenever a pilot changes aircraft or roles, the flying appointment will be preceded by ground school. Modern aircraft and today's congested airspace demand a pilot with a firm grasp of the technical complexities of his aircraft, and the complicated operating procedures involved in flying them. The BFT Ground School provides a bedrock of knowledge upon which later practical experience is built. Everything taught in Ground School is relevant to later flying, and much of it is essential knowledge. As the RAF emphasizes, a lack of application on the part of the student at this stage is considered unprofessional and will not go unnoticed, inevitably reflecting badly on

his assessment as a potential military pilot.

■ **Mass Briefings.** Most new phases of flying at BFT are preceded by a Mass Brief, given by one of the FTS Qualified Flying Instructors (QFI). The students will not receive another instructional briefing before flying the appropriate sorties, and so it is essential that the student listen and understand, making written notes of important points.

■ **Simulator/Cockpit Procedures Trainer (CPT).** Some flying exercises will be preceded by a sortie in a simulator, an invaluable opportunity to learn and practise techniques that will later be used in the air. The student is expected to prepare for a simulator sortie as though it were a real flight. Naturally, the simulator cannot provide a totally convincing airborne environment, and the students are always only too well aware that they are on the ground. But the simulator is a valuable tool for learning procedures and improving one's capability to deal with a variety of sometimes confusing visual and audible inputs.

■ **The Student Handbook.** This document covers all the major points relevant to each exercise in the BFT course. The appropriate section must be read and mentally noted by the student prior to the pre-flight briefing.

■ **The Pre-Flight Brief.** Immediately before each

Left: A hint of the unusual flying attitudes associated with low flying, as seen through the windscreen of a Dominie navigational trainer. This view is obtained at 500 feet, whereas much of the flying training syllabus on the Tucano and Hawk will be flown at just 250 feet.

Right: Three pictures showing the familiar shape of a Jet Provost T5, taxiing back on to the flightline at RAF Linton-on-Ouse in Yorkshire. The Jet Provost finally left RAF service in 1992, when flying training at 1FTS (at Linton) transferred to the Tucano. However, although the aircraft type has changed, the training schedules have remained essentially the same.

sortie the instructor will brief his student on the flight, to remind him of the basic outline of the sortie and the techniques to be learned. No new points will be introduced or discussed at this stage.

■ **The Sortie.** All the elements of preparation and rehearsal come together in the airborne sortie. The student is expected to watch the instructor's demonstrations and use the techniques that he teaches, even at the expense of accuracy, which will come later.

■ **The Post-Flight De-Brief.** The instructor discusses the flight, and analyses what, if anything, went wrong. The de-brief tends to focus upon bad points, in order to learn from mistakes, and the instructors dutifully note the parts that went well without further discussion.

■ **Private Study.** Following the de-brief, the students are encouraged to consider the points raised, noting lessons that have been learned and attempting to improve knowledge and capability, ready for the next sortie.

These are the formal elements of instruction, but the student will also have ample opportunity to talk informally with his instructor and other students, in the crew room. As the RAF emphasizes, the more work done on the ground before each flight, the easier the sortie becomes. By not using most of one's mental capacity remembering the basics, more attention can be devoted to learning and mastering new techniques. Flying demands quick thinking from the outset and the student must be free to concentrate on his task without irrelevant distractions. He must also be made to feel that he is the subject of what the RAF calls 'benevolent discipline', and instructors

make every effort to ensure that discomforts, doubts and extraneous worries are minimal. Careful attention on the part of the instructor is amply rewarded by trust and respect from the student.

So, having looked at the concepts of the Royal Air Force's Basic Flying Training syllabus, it is time to become acquainted with the Shorts Tucano. Preparation for the sortie begins the night before. It is important to get sufficient sleep. Professional pilots don't drink and socialize all night, despite their 'macho' image. High spirits have to be reserved for the weekend, as military flying is a demanding profession that requires above-average fitness and absolute dedication.

Reading the Student Study Guide will tell the student what to expect, and what preparations need to be made. Particularly during later parts of the course, a great deal needs to be done, such as map preparation, route study, low-level airspace bookings, flight planning checks and weather forecasts. It will be the student's responsibility to accommodate all these requirements. As part of this self-briefing he should check every item of his flying equipment; he will need to have Flight Reference Cards, an En-Route Supplement and Flight Information Handbook, an En-Route chart, a Local Area Map (1:500,000) and a Kneepad Chart with a Tacan (Tactical Air Navigation) overlay.

It is also the student's responsibility to ensure that his flying clothing is serviceable; deciding what kit to wear is often a difficult balance between survival and comfort. It is important to ensure that no personal effects are taken into the cockpit. Clothing should always be checked for pens, loose change, keys and any other items that could come loose in flight. If anything is lost in the cockpit it should be reported immediately so that a thorough search can be made; until the object is found the aircraft will not be cleared to fly. It takes courage to admit one's mistakes, but embarrassment is a small price to pay for a clear conscience. Lives have been lost because aircraft controls have been jammed by foreign objects.

The pre-flight brief will be given by an instructor, the student listening carefully, making a note of specific tasks on his kneepad. Following the brief, the instructor will enter details of the flight in an authorization sheet. The final action before walking to the aircraft is to read through the out-brief. This is a last-minute check-list of the important things that should have been done; a 'safety net' designed to catch omissions of planning or authorization before it is too late. As the

Above: Hawk T1A climbing away from RAF Chivenor, wearing the markings of the now-defunct 63 (Reserve) Squadron.

Right: Plan view of a pair of 4FTS Hawks, over the coastline of Wales.

student does this, he notes the following information on his kneepad: slot number and landing time; captain's callsign; diversion details and minimum landing fuel; base weather and information code; aircraft number.

After out-briefing it is time to collect the remaining items of flying clothes, such as leg restraint garters, life-jacket and helmet. The details concerning aircraft limitations, acceptable faults, maintenance and servicing are all scrutinized by the instructor, before signing to accept the aircraft. When this task has been completed, the instructor and student walk out on to the flight line, towards the assigned aircraft.

Once the appropriate tail number and serial is located, a careful check should be made that all unnecessary ground equipment has been placed within designated 'safe' areas, and that the aircraft is parked in a sensible position away from buildings and obstructions. On a recognized flight line there should be no such problems, but on an unfamiliar airfield the aircraft may have been positioned without sufficient taxiing space, and it should be moved before strap-in and start-up. The crew check that wheel chocks are in position and that a fire extinguisher is readily available, also that there are no obvious signs of

fuel or hydraulic leaks. External walk-round checks should then be made, as shown in detail by your instructor. Once these are complete, instructor and student can climb aboard, strap in, and start the engine.

Sortie 1

This is the student's first flight in a Tucano. Although he will have flown before, he may well find that the Tucano is quite different from his previous aircraft, be it a Cessna, Chipmunk or Bulldog. Completely unfamiliar surroundings are not the ideal learning environment, and this is why the first sortie includes no formal instruction. The purpose of this sortie is to accustom the student to the sights, sounds and smells of the Tucano. The instructor will be aware of the student's previous flying experience and he will

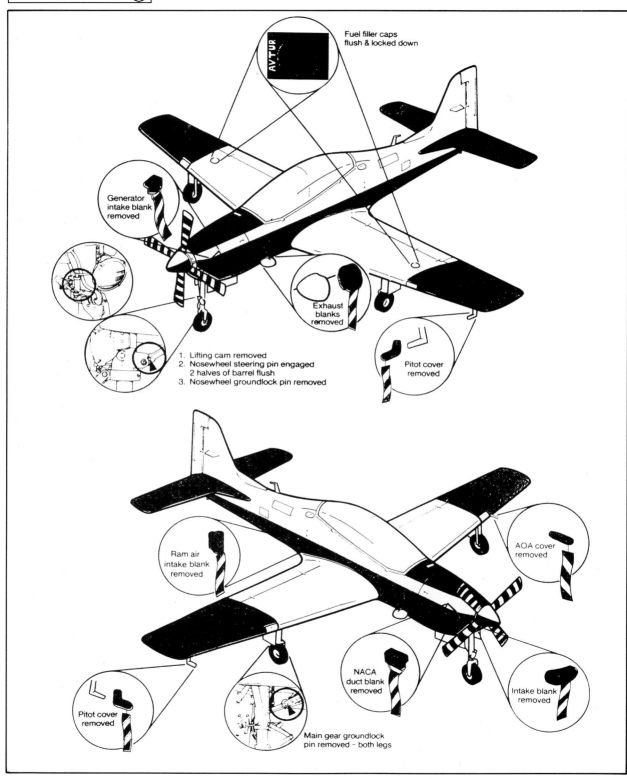

Fuel filler caps
flush & locked down

AVTUR

Generator
intake blank
removed

Exhaust
blanks
removed

Pitot cover
removed

1. Lifting cam removed
2. Nosewheel steering pin engaged
   2 halves of barrel flush
3. Nosewheel groundlock pin removed

Ram air
intake blank
removed

AOA cover
removed

Pitot cover
removed

NACA
duct blank
removed

Intake blank
removed

Main gear groundlock
pin removed - both legs

plan the sortie to take this into account. Whenever possible the sortie will be flown in weather conditions that permit the student to see the ground, and the instructor will point out the most prominent local features, towns and airfields. This sortie will also be a good opportunity to assess the comfort of flying clothing; if the student is uncomfortable in the air, he will be less able to absorb instruction. This sortie is unassessed, but the student's reaction may be an indicator to his future progress.

Sortie 2

This is the student's first full instructional sortie. The aims of the flight are to teach the student to select, and trim the aircraft to, a specific attitude, to achieve and maintain straight and level flight in trim, at cruise power, and to teach the effects on trim of changing power and speed. The instructor will try to make the trip as enjoyable as possible in order to motivate the student and fire his enthusiasm for flying the Tucano. As the student will already have some flying experience, he should understand the effects of the primary flying controls, although the Tucano will be much more responsive than anything he has flown before, and operate over a much wider speed range.

Sortie 3

On the previous flight the student learned to achieve trimmed straight and level flight at cruise

power, and to control the aircraft while changing power. On this sortie the student will develop his skill to maintain straight and level flight while accelerating and decelerating, learning to achieve and maintain any speed within the Tucano's range. He will also learn to turn on to selected headings, using 30 degrees of bank. To maintain cruise speed in the Tucano, about 40% of torque (Tq) is required, i.e., at 180 knots, a setting of 40% Tq gives just enough thrust to balance drag. To accelerate, the torque must be increased in order to produce more thrust than drag, but as airspeed increases, so does drag. For example, increasing speed from 180kt to 220kt increases drag by about 45%, requiring an increase in torque to 68%. Naturally it would be possible to accelerate to the new speed by simply setting the new power required, but as the acceleration would be so slow, in practice the student should apply more power than required, and as the target speed is approached the power should be reduced to that required to maintain the speed.

Sortie 4

By this stage the student should be able to fly the Tucano at a selected speed, and be able to turn using 30 degrees of bank. Sortie No. 4 applies these skills to maintaining straight and level flight while operating ancillary services (landing gear, flap and airbrake), fundamental skills required to fly the downwind leg of an airfield circuit. When these skills have been mastered, the instructor

Right: Jet Provost T3A, an aircraft which served the Royal Air Force for many years. The majority of current operational RAF pilots received their basic training on this aircraft.

The Training

Top left: Instructor's-eye view of tail-chasing in the Tucano.

Left: The Shorts Tucano, proudly wearing the blue fuselage band of No 3 FTS, RAF Cranwell.

Above: Climbing away over the 3FTS flightline at RAF Cranwell.

will teach the student how to join the airfield circuit and, weather permitting, practise the whole sequence in the circuit.

Sortie 5

The student can now maintain a climb and descent, and now he is taught to enter, and level-off from, a climb and descent. His manoeuvring skills are also extended by learning how to make level turns at 45 degrees, while maintaining a speed of 180kt. This is not a particularly 'busy' sortie, and it allows the student some time to consolidate previous exercises.

Sorties 6 and 7

The remaining skills necessary to fly an airfield circuit are now taught, and the instructor demonstrates a final approach to the runway. Additionally the instructor will demonstrate a full, clean stall, in preparation for the next sortie (7). The student will see that the Tucano behaves well in the stall, and it is neither a violent nor unpleasant manoeuvre. But a great deal of height can be lost in a stall and this would be disastrous in the airfield circuit. Consequently it is essential that

the student recognize the symptoms of an approaching stall and is able to recover from the situation. Normally it should be the student's aim to fly the Tucano so that the possibility of an inadvertent stall never arises, but stalling practice will continue throughout the FTS courses, in all configurations.

Closing the throttle and maintaining straight and level flight will naturally decrease airspeed. This itself is a warning that the aircraft is approaching the stall angle. As the speed drops it is necessary to raise the nose until, at slow speeds, a high nose attitude is required to maintain level flight. The angle of attack (AOA) increases steadily, and as the speed reduces the controls will feel less responsive. Finally, the audio stall warning will sound, followed by a light buffeting through the control column. If all these warning signs are ignored the aircraft will enter a full stall. The first indication will be an increase in buffeting which will be felt throughout the airframe. The nose will drop at the stall, the aircraft will sink, and it may roll. To recover, the control column is held centrally forward until the buffeting stops, and full power is applied. All stall recoveries assume the worst case scenario, with the aircraft close to the ground, and so the aim is always to recover with minimum height loss. There is no point in successfully unstalling the aircraft if you fly into the ground during the recovery. Without question the safest recovery is the one initiated before onset of a full stall.

Sortie 8

While returning to the airfield on the previous sortie, the student will have been introduced to aerobatics. The choice and range of manoeuvres depends upon the instructor's assessment of the student's 'stomach', however, and only basic manoeuvres are demonstrated. On this next sortie the aerobatics exercises are taught to the student, aiming to make the experience as enjoyable as possible. Stalling practice continues, as does circuit flying.

Sorties 9–12

By this stage the student should have learned all the skills necessary to fly a safe airfield circuit. This block of four flights gives him time to concentrate on putting together all the skills, within the restricted environment of the airfield circuit, culminating in the student's first solo flight. The decision to send a student solo is probably the most subjective in flying training. The only rule is that of safety, and certainly the

student should be able to fly the circuit without any critical errors. A good guide is that the student should fly three consecutive circuits without any assistance, and in safety. The first solo must be supervised visually from the control tower or caravan, by the QFI who sends him solo.

Although the potential hazards of sending a student solo before he is properly fit are obvious, and will at best cause the student to lose self-confidence, if the first solo is delayed unnecessarily by the QFI's indecision, the result is often a deterioration in flying skill and the student's confidence is again likely to suffer. A successful first solo flight gives the student a well-deserved sense of achievement and added confidence, and this is often reflected in an improvement in his flying ability. Before the student is sent solo, the QFI must be satisfied that he can recognize and correct critical errors, and can react promptly and correctly to an emergency. Polished flying cannot be expected at this stage, but he must be considered safe.

The following points are used by the QFI as a guide to the required standards for a first solo:

■ **Airmanship.** The student should maintain an adequate lookout without being prompted. He must have sufficient capacity to maintain an effective RT listening watch, and to maintain an awareness of other circuit traffic; there must be no doubt about his ability to avoid other aircraft in

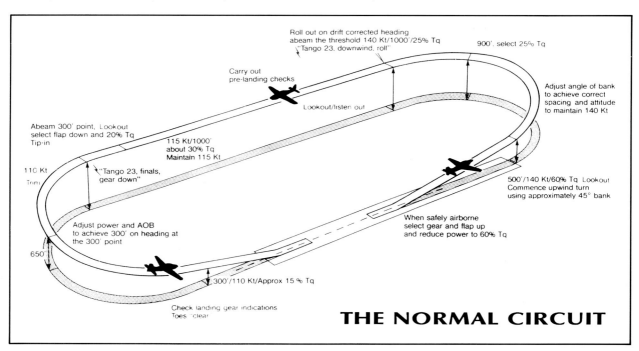

Roll out on drift corrected heading
abeam the threshold 140 Kt/1000'/25% Tq
"Tango 23, downwind, roll"

900', select 25% Tq

Carry out
pre-landing checks

Adjust angle of bank
to achieve correct
spacing and attitude
to maintain 140 Kt

Lookout/listen out

Abeam 300' point, Lookout
select flap down and 20% Tq
Tip-in

115 Kt/1000'
about 30% Tq
Maintain 115 Kt

110 Kt
Trim

"Tango 23, finals, gear down"

500'/140 Kt/60% Tq Lookout
Commence upwind turn
using approximately 45° bank

Adjust power and AOB
to achieve 300' on heading at
the 300' point

When safely airborne
select gear and flap up
and reduce power to 60% Tq

650'

300'/110 Kt/Approx 15% Tq

Check landing gear indications
Toes clear

THE NORMAL CIRCUIT

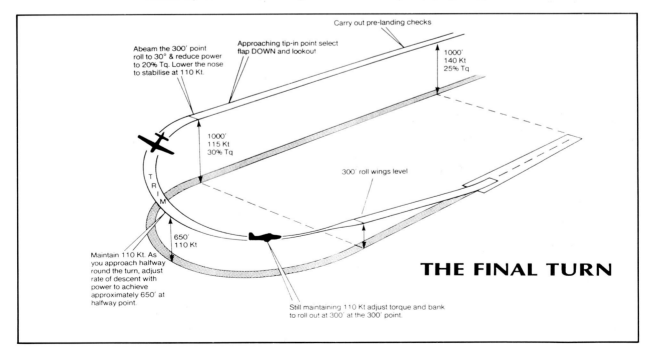

Above: Jet Provost T5, the pressurized version of the T3, proudly wearing the blue fuselage band markings signifying allocation to RAF Cranwell. The last Jet Provosts left Cranwell in 1992.

the circuit. His RT procedures must be correct, and all checks and drills must be faultless. He must be able to 'go around' safely if his approach and landing is baulked.

■ **Take-off and Climb.** The take-off must be safe. He must be able to keep straight on the take-off run, and be able to carry out the checks during take-off. He should unstick at the correct airspeed (+10kt/ −0kt) and the initial climb must be at a safe angle.

■ **Circuit.** The student must be able to produce a consistently safe circuit, although there will be

errors of flying accuracy at this stage. He must be aware of the wind and be able to compensate its effects in the circuit. He must display a high level of speed awareness and take prompt action if the speed falls below the target speed at any stage in the circuit. He must observe the 45-degree maximum bank angle limitation in the circuit.

■ **Final Approach.** The student must be able to fly a steady final approach at a safe approach angle. He should be able to control the speed accurately to +10kt/−0kt. He must be able to recognize a poorly judged approach and take action on his

THE FINAL TURN

Carry out pre-landing checks

Abeam the 300' point roll to 30° & reduce power to 20% Tq. Lower the nose to stabilise at 110 Kt.

Approaching tip-in point select flap DOWN and lookout

1000' 140 Kt 25% Tq

1000' 115 Kt 30% Tq

300' roll wings level

650' 110 Kt

Maintain 110 Kt. As you approach halfway round the turn, adjust rate of descent with power to achieve approximately 650' at halfway point.

Still maintaining 110 Kt adjust torque and bank to roll out at 300' at the 300' point.

Left: Line astern, behind a Hawk T1, looking up through the Hawk's canopy MDC.

Right: Gear down, a Tucano making a finals turn to RAF Barkston Heath, Cranwell's Relief Landing Ground (RLG).

Right: Just getting airborne, as the Tucano lifts gently from Cranwell's runway.

own initiative to go around when necessary.

■ **Landing.** Although his landings may be firm, they must be safe with no consistent faults such as holding-off too high, closing the throttle prematurely, or flying on without rounding-out. The student must be able to control the direction during the landing ground run.

■ **Emergencies.** The student must have passed Part One of the Essential Knowledge Quiz, and must have been briefed on the action to take in the event of an engine failure.

■ **Confidence.** The QFI should have noted and taken steps to correct any tendency towards over/ under confidence during pre-solo instruction. A confident student should be able to keep calm and react sensibly to unusual situations while remaining aware of his limitations. When the student is ready for solo he should be able to make safe any reasonable corrections on his own initiative, and should handle the aircraft responsibly.

After the euphoria of his first solo, the student

now needs to improve the accuracy of his circuit flying and build up his self-confidence when flying solo. From this stage in the syllabus, sorties are a mix of dual and solo configurations, with dual flights continuing for demonstrations of new skills, and solo flights for the student to gain experience and confidence. Sortie 14 develops the skills required to fly glide circuits, necessary in the event of an engine failure. Additionally, his repertoire of aerobatics is extended. Sortie 15 begins with fifteen minutes flown dual, followed by the student's first full hour flying around the airfield circuit. This includes some PFLs (Practice Forced Landing).

Sorties 16 and 17 (dual and solo respectively) give the student his first opportunity to fly solo away from the airfield circuit. Although he should be competent to fix his location and find his way home using the on-base Tacan, the QFI must also ensure that he has a good grasp of local area landmarks. At this stage the QFI also demonstrates a spin and how to recover from it. Beginning with the dual sortie, a 20-minute 'sector recce' is flown, flying point-to-point between suitable prominent landmarks, the QFI emphasizing the heading and distance to base from each landmark. After this flight (which

Above: Student climbing into the cockpit for a solo flight, in this case, in a Jet Provost T5. The side-by-side seating is missed by many instructors, who liked to see exactly what the student was doing. On the other hand, the Tucano's tandem seating is much more representative of the Hawk, Tornado and EFA which the student will later fly.

Left: Taxiing to the runway, clear visor down, tinted visor up, with the canopy still open. The instructor's seat is empty, signifying a solo flight.

Right: On completion of the sortie the student signs the Form 700, handing responsibility for the aircraft back to the servicing team.

Below: Just inches from the concrete as a Jet Provost makes a smooth approach to the runway on a gloomy winter's morning.

includes spin demonstrations and aerobatics), the student then flies for one hour solo, on his pre-determined route, keeping clear of cloud, and in sight of the ground at all times, flying at 2,000ft or higher. Once back at home base, the student flies more airfield circuits.

Sortie 19 will be the student's second solo flight away from the circuit, and on the previous (dual) flight the QFI will have demonstrated how to fly a diversion to the usual Crash Diversion airfield (Barkston Heath, in the case of Cranwell). He will have also demonstrated a spin entry and recovery. This is the most important part of Sortie 18, but it is also the part most likely to 'upset' the student. Consequently the QFI leaves this until the end of the flight, first demonstrating the Crash Diversion, then climbing for steep turns and 'emergency breaks', before covering spinning. The student may be apprehensive about spinning, and the QFI will begin by teaching recovery at the incipient stage before progressing to the full spin.

Spinning again features in the syllabus at Sortie 23, when the QFI demonstrates an inverted spin entry and recovery. The student will again be apprehensive, and it is important for the QFI to assure him that it is a pleasant manoeuvre with prompt recovery. It is also important to ensure

The Training

that the student is familiar with the difference between an erect and inverted spin and is able to identify both. The series of spin flights is completed with Sortie 25, during which the student also flies more aerobatics and learns how to fly an approach and landing without extended flaps. This manoeuvre will have first been demonstrated prior to the student's first solo, and so it is now flown again by the student with verbal assistance from the QFI.

The following sorties are a gradual move towards the Progress Test, at Sortie 29. This is a test by the supervisory staff to assess the student's progress to date, and his ability to manage a

Left: QFI (left) and student in front of their Hawk T1, at RAF Valley.

simple GH (General Handling) sortie. The student will be expected to plan and manage the sortie on his own, but he may need some advice from the QFI as to the best sequence to fly the different exercises and the best area in which to operate. The test outline is:

■ **Take-off.** Climb to a suitable area for GH.

■ **Steep Turns.**

■ **Stalling.** Clean configuration, fully developed. Approach configuration, incipient in the final turn.

■ **Spinning.** One erect spin, one inverted spin, each of at least four turns.

■ **Aerobatics.** Loop, aileron roll and roll off the

Right: The BAe Bulldog T1 primary trainer, used by the Royal Air Force's University Air Squadrons (UASs).

The Training

Left: The Tucano's propeller is certainly eye-catching, and deliberately so. Wit generations of RAF air and ground crews having become accustomed to jet aircraft, the RAF felt it was vital to emphasize the dangers of working near propellers. The black/white markings tend to draw attention to the turning blades.

top of a loop. Barrell roll, left and right.

■ **Visual UPs.** Recovering from UPs (Unusual Positions). Incipient spin off manoeuvre, erect and inverted. Recovery from the vertical with low speed and high Tq. Near inverted position, with nose below the horizon. Mishandled barrel roll.

■ **Simulated Emergency.** Leading to a visual Practice Forced Landing.

■ **Circuit.** Normal circuit. Glide, flapless, low level. At a convenient stage the examiner will initiate a practice crash diversion.

This is a 'pass-or-fail' test, but if the student does not pass he can be given additional flying training before flying the test again. Additional hours can be given to each student, if required, to compensate for times during the course when the student encounters difficulty. But this is an important point in the syllabus, which the student must complete in order to proceed further. Failing to 'make the grade' at this point would mean 'the chop' (termination of flying training). There are nine Critical Points (CPs) in the training syllabus,

Above: Close-up of the Tucano's nose gear assembly.

Above right: Close-up of the Tucano's port main undercarriage, with the locking pin in place (with 'remove before flight' flag attached).

where the student reaches a 'pass-or-fail' point, each representing a key point in the programme.

The following sorties begin to concentrate more on IF (Instrument Flying), teaching the student to use the Tucano's flight instruments, rather than just his visual skills. The instruction leads towards the next Critical Point, the BIFGT – Basic Instrument Flying Grading Test. This test includes the following points:

■ **Instrument Take-Off.**
■ **Standard Instrument Departure – Tacan.**
■ **Climbing Turns.** On to nominated headings.
■ **Scanex.** Climbing, descending and turning at nominated speeds, to specified flight levels and headings.
■ **Steep Turn.** In each direction through at least 180 degrees, using 60 degrees of bank.
■ **Recovery From UPs.** To straight and level flight using main and standby Attitude Indicator (AI). From: approaching the stall; near vertical; spiral dive.
■ **Tacan Recovery.** Using the main Attitude Indicator.
■ **Oral Test.** Of knowledge of relevant ATC (Air Traffic Control) procedures.

Following the BIFG Test the student flies some general handling revision, much of his time now being devoted to 'applied' skills, and his GH ability may begin to deteriorate unless it is maintained. The syllabus then turns to navigation, and by this stage the student will have already been using many of the basic principles of navigation, possibly without even realizing it. The first navigation phase formalizes the situation and teaches basic visual navigation, followed by radio aids navigation. The first sortie (No. 42) covers the principles of visual/low-level navigation, flown in sight of the ground, between 1,000ft and 3,000ft. By this stage in the course the student will already be familiar with planning and map preparation, map orientation, simple map reading and the use of large features, estimation of headings and distances, and an 'activity cycle'. However, the QFI will still assist him with map preparation, choice of features, and calculations.

Instrument flying continues, leading to the AIFGT (Advanced Instrument Flying Grading Test), following which the student is introduced to the low-level flying environment, the QFI demonstrating how visually to judge heights of 500ft and 250ft. The sortie (No. 55) is completed with a demonstration of what to do following a birdstrike at low level. Teaching a student how to assess and maintain low-level heights can be

Left: The RAF uses the 'clock reporting system', to locate other aircraft visually. Assuming that we are looking at an imaginary clock face, the two Hawks are visible in our 10 o'clock position.

done within the airfield circuit, but the flat and empty picture presented by an airfield is better replaced by flying through operating areas where there is a good variety of ground features. Students tend to creep progressively lower while flying straight and level, but tend to climb when turning, and the QFI tries to 'iron out' this tendency. During Sortie 56 the techniques of visual navigation and low-level flying are combined for the first time, progressing to a combination of high- and low-level navigation on Sortie 59.

Sorties 63 and 64 are flown back-to-back, with a refuelling stop in between at another airfield (a land-away). The range of skills being exercised by the student continues to increase, flying on instruments, or visually, at high and low level, while still flying GH exercises from time to time. Sortie 71 introduces the student to night flying, and although the instructor will assure the student that night flying is no more difficult than flying in daylight, the environment is obviously unfamiliar and the student must familiarize himself with night flying before going solo.

Sortie 80 is the introduction to formation flying, another important aspect of military operations. All basic formation phase flights are flown as three-ship formations. The high degree of concentration required during formation sorties is extremely tiring, and the QFI will take over the controls from time to time so as to give the student an opportunity to relax. However the student will

only learn by practice, albeit with verbal assistance, and so he is encouraged to handle the controls as much as possible. He may become disorientated when the horizon is obscured, and to combat this the QFI will try to teach him to trust the leader, maintaining an accurate formation position, but trying to relax as much as possible while remaining mentally alert. The complexity of each sortie increases, introducing formation take-offs, tail-chasing, stream take-offs, formation turns and formation breaks over the airfield.

Each and every skill included in the syllabus so far is practised time and time again until the student reaches sortie 100, the Intermediate Handling Test, at which stage the RAF will establish whether the student has made sufficient progress to be selected for an appropriate lead-in course for fast jets, multi-engines, or helicopters. The sortie outline is:

■ **Take-Off.** And climb.
■ **Steep Turns.**
■ **Maximum Rate Turns.**
■ **Maximum Possible Rate Turns.**
■ **Stalling.** Clean and approach, full or incipient recovery including a simulated finals turn.
■ **Spinning.** Two spins, one erect, one inverted, at least four turns in each. Spin off a manoeuvre. An incipient spin.
■ **Aerobatics.** Basic aerobatics in a loosely linked sequence flown to a base height.

Right: Rushing over the bleak countryside at 480 knots, looking through the Hawk's gunsight.

■ **Low Flying.** General Handling and a short pre-planned leg.

■ **Simulated Emergency.**

■ **Practice Diversion.**

■ **Tacan/Radar Practice Forced Landing** through a simulated cloud layer.

■ **Circuits.** Normal, Glide, Flapless and Low level.

The overall pass/fail decision is at the discretion of the testing officer, and deciding which lead-in course the student should be selected for is a subjective matter, chiefly depending on the experience of the instructors. There are no specific rules to dictate which of the three paths would best suit each student, but for those who are selected to fly fast jets, the QFIs are often looking for 'safe aggressiveness', good reactions under pressure, and generally someone who is 'switched on'. Some students are simply unsuited to this environment. Their instrument flying skills may be excellent, but it may be that they cannot fly accurately at low level, or may need more time to make sound decisions. This kind of student is a better choice for multi-engines or helicopters.

The students selected for the Fast Jet Lead-in course continue Tucano flying, with Sortie 106 being an Instrument Rating Test (IRT), from which the successful student will be awarded an Amber Instrument Rating. General Handling and navigation exercises continue, and whenever possible during the Fast Jet Lead-in course, aircraft operate as pairs, slowly building upon the student's ability in every aspect of the flying syllabus. The final sorties of the course prepare the student for Sortie 132, the Final Handling Test (FHT). It will have been some considerable time since the student has flown a GH sortie, so the QFI devotes sorties 127–131 to 'final polishing' of overall performance. Captaincy, airmanship and sortie management bear heavily on the final result, so particular attention is paid to these qualities. The content of each sortie will be tailored to the individual needs of each student. He will be given a series of tasks, and then left to plan and present the sortie. Suggested contents for the final three dual sorties are:

Sortie 127.

■ Circuits.

■ Spinning and Stalling.

■ Aerobatic Sequence.

■ Steep and Max Rate Turns.

■ Simulated Emergencies.

■ Practice Diversion to Crash Div.

Sortie 130.

■ Circuits.

■ Low Flying.

■ Aerobatic Sequence.

■ Max. Possible Rate Turns.

■ Simulated Emergencies.

■ Radar/Tacan Practice Forced Landing.

Left: Tucano's port wing, showing the pitot head assembly and wingtip navigation lights.

Right: The starboard wing of the Tucano, illustrating the aileron and associated trim tab. Also visible are static discharge wings on the extreme edge of the aileron.

Right: Tucano's starboard fuselage, emphasizing the seating arrangement, in which the instructor sits slightly higher than the student, affording a good view over his head. The Central Flying School's emblem is on the fuselage, indicating that this Tucano is used to teach instructors.

Sortie 131.
- FHT-Type Profile:
- Max and Max Possible Rate Turns.
- Spinning Erect and Inverted.
- Aerobatic Sequence.
- Simulated Emergency With Diversion.
- Practice Forced Landing.
- Circuits.

Sorties 128 and 129 are flown solo, allowing the student to practise all aspects of handling except spinning and low flying. The sorties may be linked with a land-away. The student is encouraged to analyse his own performance and to so plan his solo sorties as to extract the most benefit. The QFI monitors his chosen profiles, and modifies them where necessary, based on the QFI's assessment of the student's needs. And finally the student reaches the FHT, the test outline of which may cover any exercise from the whole syllabus, but must include the following:

- Max and Max Possible Rate Turns.
- Spinning – From Manoeuvre and Incipient.
- Aerobatic Sequence.
- Simulated Emergency.
- Practice Diversion.
- Practice Forced Landing.
- Circuits.

In total, a student can expect to spend 46 weeks on the Tucano course, with roughly five

Above: Tucano's port fuselage, the canopy unlocked. The flaps are slightly extended. Also visible is the canopy miniature detonating chord (MDC), which will shatter the canopy prior to the two ejection seats firing.

Below: The Tucano's starboard flap, slightly extended, with two static discharge wicks attached.

and a decision was made to combine these stages into a common syllabus, divided between two bases. Initially, the change has caused many observers to question whether the RAF is lowering standards to some degree, as one direct result of the new syllabus is a reduction in flying hours. But 4FTS and 7FTS staff are eager to point out that almost all the reductions in flying hours have been achieved by 'pruning' sorties that were unnecessary.

The students who do succeed in reaching either Valley or Chivenor will, at last, begin flying training on a combat-capable 'fast jet'. The aim of the early phases of the 4/7FTS course is to develop the student pilot's skills in operating a high-performance aircraft in tactical situations, a kind of 'half-way house' between basic flying training and tactical weapons training. They will be taught how to fly and navigate at high speed and low level. Exercises are divided into 'convex' (conversion exercise) phases, where the student learns to handle and operate the Hawk in a variety of situations, and an 'applied' phase, where he flies the Hawk 'for a specific purpose', following pre-determined routes around the UK. The skills acquired at this stage are vital in order to ensure successful completion of the later phases of the course, when the student will be expected to operate the Hawk almost as second nature, and to be able to concentrate on the tactical and operational aspects of military fast-jet flying.

Because pilot training is so expensive, the BFTS QFIs will have 'weeded-out' almost everyone who is unlikely to succeed at Valley or Chivenor, so the 'survivors' stand a good chance of making the grade. But 4FTS has long had a formidable reputation, and approximately 20–25% of each intake is likely to be 'chopped' at some stage. Consequently the Tucano graduates arrive with great trepidation, as they settle into the first couple of weeks of Ground School. Those that do fail at this stage usually reveal an incapacity to cope with the Hawk's cockpit workload, which is greater than that of the Tucano, and while there is always a reluctance to 'chop' any student, the QFIs emphasize that there is little point in pushing the student through the course, only to have him fail at a later stage. Generally, if a student flies three consecutive poor sorties, he will be placed 'on review', meaning that his progress will be monitored more carefully, and that he will fly with the most experienced instructors, even being given additional flying hours if it is thought necessary. If he still doesn't improve, the Squad-

Above: The tail assembly of the Tucano, illustrating the rudder and trib tab. The port tailplane also incorporates a trim tab, but the starboard tailplane does not have one.

hours of flying in each week of the flying elements. Successfully negotiating the entire course, however, does not qualify the student to fly front-line combat aircraft. From the BFTS he (or she) will move to one of two RAF stations: RAF Valley on the island of Anglesey (No. 4 Flying Training School) or RAF Chivenor in Devon (No. 7 Flying Training School). These two bases operate 'mirror-image' FTSs which take the student through advanced and tactical training to a point at which he is ready to join an Operational Conversion Unit (OCU) flying a combat aircraft type.

The advanced/tactical system is a relatively new set-up for the RAF, having been first introduced in 1992. Until then the RAF had sent all students to 4FTS for advanced flying training, after which they moved to one of two Tactical Weapons Units, where their skills were first applied in the air defence and ground-attack environment. However, drastic defence cuts prompted the RAF to re-appraise training needs,

Left: The Tucano's front cockpit where the student will learn the basics of flying.

ron Commander will fly with the student, and decide whether or not to recommend that the student be 'chopped'. If such a recommendation is made, the student flies with the FTS Chief Flying Instructor, who will ultimately decide whether the student should be suspended from training. Most students tend to respond to such 'intensive care' and eventually return to the normal syllabus.

So what is it like to fly on a typical Hawk sortie? The author visited RAF Valley on a cold and blustery day to see, first-hand, what Hawk flying is all about. The first task of the day is to visit the Station Medical Officer, who ensures that all Hawk passengers are fit and well, and capable of safely withstanding the rigours of fast-jet flying.

The attentions of the MO might seem a little over-zealous, but even the briefest of conversations with a physician will reveal what a potentially lethal environment the cockpit of a fast jet really is. There are, as you are regularly told, many ways in which you could easily meet with an untimely demise, and a combat aircraft has to be treated with the greatest respect. From a medical point of view, it is naturally important to be free from respiratory or circulatory problems and other obvious ailments. But even the common cold will prohibit flying, as the changes in air pressure caused by rapid ascent or descent will lead to perforated ear drums, if one's nose is blocked. Likewise, even something so mundane as one's arm and leg length can be important; not

Above: The instructor's rear cockpit in the Tucano, essentially a repeat of the front cockpit's layout. The leg restraint lanyards are wrapped around the control column for convenience.

too short so as to be unable to reach every control in the cockpit, but not too long either, or one might break one's legs in the event of having to eject. And of course one might simply be too big to fit into the cockpit. Many considerations have to be taken into account, and it is little wonder that the RAF sends even 'occasional passengers' such as journalists to their Central Medical Establishment in London, and the Aviation Medicine Training Centre at North Luffenham, for examination and instruction before they are permitted to fly in any high-performance aircraft.

Once the MO has signed the appropriate clearance, the next stop is a visit to the Flying Clothing Section, where the peculiar and rather uncomfortable clothing is fitted. Starting with the 'easy' items, a pair of woollen (fire-resistant and warm) socks is issued, together with the comical long-johns underwear. Over this goes an olive green sweatshirt and flying overalls – also olive-green and fire-resistant, with Velcro adjustments and zip pockets. The sturdy boots complete the basic attire, although for winter/cold weather operations there would be the added 'pleasure' of squeezing into the infamous 'goon suit', a rubber immersion suit which is immensely uncomfort-

able, hot and almost impossible to get in and out of. However, its protective qualities in an ice-cold sea are undeniable. Next comes the anti-g trousers, the 'g-suit' as it is commonly known. This garment slips over the flying overalls and is zipped into place before being adjusted to fit as snugly as possible. The fit has to be fairly tight so that, when attached to the air system in the Hawk, the trousers' inflatable bladders will effectively squeeze one's stomach and legs, slowing the drain of blood from one's brain during a high-g manoeuvre. The g-suit isn't a perfect 'cure-all', but it does give the wearer something like 1g's-worth of extra tolerance.

Next is the flying helmet, a heavy and cumbersome piece of equipment, which again has to fit as tightly as possible. A loose-fitting helmet would be particularly dangerous in an ejection. Once the helmet has been pushed and squeezed into place, a technician will adjust its internal cradle to fit snugly, before attaching an oxygen mask and tube which will be tested for correct functioning prior to issue. Finally, a standard life-jacket, a pair of leg restraint garters and flying gloves complete the clothing. It has already been a long day and we have yet to go flying!

Suitably equipped, we now join the pre-flight briefing, where the aims of the sortie are outlined and the planned route is examined. Heights, speeds, timings, diversions, weather, callsigns, fuel — all important considerations which everybody needs to understand. Naturally a journalist observer doesn't have any major input into the briefing, but as a passenger in the Hawk it is vital to know exactly what is going on and what everybody is doing. The briefing complete, it is time to collect helmets, life-jackets, maps and gloves, and head for the flight line, stopping en route to scrutinise the aircraft's log book and sign to accept the Hawk for our sortie. Then out to the aircraft to conduct a careful walk-round inspection of the airframe before climbing aboard. Attaching oneself to the Martin-Baker Mk.10 seat is a fairly complicated task for anyone unfamiliar with the procedure, but when compared with older ejection seat designs, the Hawk's seat is relatively simple because it features a combined parachute and seat harness. Once seated, the first task is to route the leg restraint lanyards carefully through the D-rings on the garters attached to one's legs. The lanyards are then plugged into sockets on the base of the seat. If the seat is fired, the lanyards will rapidly retract into the seat, snatching one's legs firmly into the base of the seat to ensure a safe ejection. Flailing limbs would be broken during the violent exit from the aircraft.

Next, I attach the PSP (Personal Survival Pack) clip, ensuring that I am attached to the dinghy and associated assortment of survival aids which are located under the seat cushion. Also at this time, the PEC connection is clicked into place. The PEC (Personal Equipment Connector) connects my oxygen mask tube to the Hawk's onboard oxygen system, ensuring that I have a flow of either pure oxygen or the normal 'airmix'. Confirmation that the system is functioning is made by checking a 'dolls-eye' on the instrument panel, which blinks from black to white every time a breath of air is taken. The PEC also supplies high-pressure air to the g-suit, and a test button is pressed to check that the bladders inflate proper-

Left: The right-hand side of the cockpit, emphasizing the uncluttered nature of the Tucano's internal layout. The bank of circuit-breakers is evident.

Right: The port side of the cockpit interior in the Tucano, illustrating the throttle lever, flap and undercarriage selection switches among other items.

ly. This done, my attention turns to the seat straps, and I thread the two leg loops through D-rings in the appropriate lap-straps. The shoulder-straps are then routed through the leg loops and pushed into the quick-release box. With the harness fixed, each strap is individually tightened, particular emphasis being placed on the lap-straps, as these will ensure that I remain attached tightly to the seat when the Hawk flies inverted or rolls, etc. Another consideration is that a sloppy lap connection will cause quite severe thigh injuries if the ejection sequence is initiated.

This done, the helmet is squeezed into place, the tightening lugs on each side being flipped into their secure position, before lowering the face visor (either clear or tinted). The visor is normally lowered before the canopy is closed, to avoid the risk of facial injury, should the MDC (Miniature Detonating Chord) malfunction, and shatter the Perspex. The oxygen mask is clipped on, the radio link is plugged in, and on go the gloves. For a passenger, the pre-flight preparations are then essentially complete. In the front cockpit (where the student would normally sit), a 4FTS instructor completes the pre-start checks, before the distinctive exhaust whistle indicates that the Hawk's internal gas turbine starter is running. The starter is clutched into the main engine mechanism, and the Rolls-Royce/Turboméca Adour 151 groans into life. Further down the flight line, our 'playmate' (another Hawk) is also ready to taxy, and a call over the RT confirms that we are also ready to go. The canopy is closed now, and the MDC

safety pin is removed and stowed next to the seat pin, which is also removed, making the Martin-Baker 10B seat live, and ready to function instantly if required. The seat has a zero-zero capability, meaning that it could, in theory, be used successfully from a standing start on the taxyway. The rear seat also has a command function which would allow an instructor to eject both himself and then the student, 0.55 seconds later.

The chocks are pulled away from the wheels, and a slight touch of power pushes forward, before the pilot squeezes the brakes (part of the rudder pedal mechanism) to check their effectiveness. Off forward again and we turn left, along the flight line, passing a long row of Hawks, to the active runway. Moving along the concrete, it quickly becomes clear that the instructor has an excellent all-round view from the Hawk's rear seat, including a superb forward view over his student's head. The differential steering is effective, although it does take time for students to learn to control accurately the Hawk's speedy taxying capabilities. At the holding point, just short of runway 32, we join our sister aircraft, and there is time for the crews to make a last-minute check of everything before lining up on the runway. Air Traffic Control gives 'Snapper One

and Snapper Two' clearance to lineup and take-off, and we take up line-abreast position – either side of the runway centreline markings.

As 'Snapper Two' rolls forward, we are briefly buffeted by the Hawk's exhaust, as the sprightly little trainer roars away ahead of us. Our throttle also goes forward, and after checking the engine RPM and TGT (Turbine Gas Temperature), the brakes are released and we surge forward, guiding the nose towards the centreline with brake pressure, and then with rudder input as the speed increases and the rudder begins to 'bite'. Acceleration is quite brisk, and at 90 knots the control column is gently pulled back, the nose rises, and at just over 120 knots we are airborne, having travelled little more than half-way down the runway. The landing gear is selected 'up', and a couple of muted thumps indicate that the gear doors have closed indicators on the instrument panel confirming retraction. Flaps are also raised quickly, before reaching their limiting speed of 200 knots, which is already fast approaching. Still climbing straight ahead, we pass over Holy Island before turning to port and formating alongside 'Snapper One'.

The two Hawks continue in formation across the southern side of Anglesey, through the low-level 'one-way' route across the Menai Strait.

Above: Direct rear view of the Tucano, illustrating the conventional airframe configuration.

and uncluttered appearance. The majority of non-flying controls are in the front cockpit, making the rear 'office' appear even more tidy, especially as this particular aircraft (XX184) is a 'standard' T1, without the HUD (Head Up Display) associated with the former Tactical Weapons Unit Hawks, and particularly the Sidewinder-capable T1A. The main attitude indicator dominates the instrument panel, with the compass immediately below it. To the left is a combined speed indicator and to the right the main altimeter.

Clear of the gloomy coastal weather, we make a slow descent over Wales, down into the hills, where we settle into the standard low-level altitude of 250ft at a speed of 360 knots, a convenient six miles per minute, which is also a useful cruising speed. Down 'on the deck' the impression of speed is, to say the least, attention-grabbing. As one pilot describes it, it is 'like driving a high-speed go-cart', and for students fresh from the Tucano the increase in speed is quite noticeable. As for the aircraft itself, the instrument panel is very similar to that of the Tucano (intentionally so, as the Tucano's instruments were designed to match the Hawk layout), and apart from the extra speed, the handling is also quite similar, although there is a longer delay between the application of power and the accompanying increase in speed. The Tucano's turbo-prop provides instant power, and students tend to forget the small time-lag associated with a jet engine. Judging the 250ft height takes practice, and to a complete novice such as myself it is very difficult to determine the precise altitude, especially in the Welsh hills, where the terrain rises and falls by the second.

The RAF would, in some circumstances, like to fly lower, not least because a realistic wartime operational height has long been regarded as being about fifty feet. Naturally it would be impossible to operate at such heights over the UK, and for training purposes such potentially lethal heights are out of the question; 250ft is regarded as being a fair compromise between the need for realism and the equally important need for safety. Additionally, the nuisance factor has to be considered, and the residents of Britain's countryside could hardly be expected to ignore fast jets flying by at anything less than 250ft. Even at this height, there's no doubting the Hawk's presence from the ground, and every effort is made to spread the low-level training over as many varying routes as possible, so as to avoid creating too much disturbance to any particular location. In fact, the resulting restrictions make

Above: The instructor's ejection seat in the Tucano.

Hawks inbound to Valley take the northern side, thus easing the congestion which would otherwise occur in this relatively small but busy region of airspace around Valley and the RLG (Relief Landing Ground) at Mona. Once over the mainland we climb through the cloud cover, and break formation, allowing us to continue our solo demonstration flight. During the outbound flight there is time to take a closer look at the Hawk's internal layout. The first impression is that there is a relatively large amount of room in the cockpit, and the instrument panel has a very clean, logical the student's low-level map look like a nightmare, littered with hundreds of 'one-way' routes, avoidance areas, restricted zones, and prohibited airspace. The RAF is permitted to fly in the spaces between all these restrictions, and in a crowded island like the UK it makes route planning very, very difficult.

For the purposes of this demonstration sortie, we take a low-level route at 420 knots, representative of the kind of speeds used towards the end of the Hawk syllabus. Navigation sorties are flown to airfields all over the UK, ranging from Chivenor in Devon, right up to Lossiemouth in Scotland. Even civilian airfields are sometimes chosen for practice diversions, to places such as Ronaldsway on the Isle of Man, or Liverpool or Blackpool. Certainly the Hawk has sufficient fuel capacity easily to reach any destination required by 4FTS. The first turning point on our route is the southern edge of Llyn Clywedog, a lake running alongside the B4518 road. I am just starting to think about looking for the feature when we turn hard over the lake, having already reached it. Unfortunately for an untrained passenger, it is very easy to forget the speed at which things happen. Heading north, we approach Llandidloes, which has to be avoided either laterally or vertically. We choose to go around the town, carefully negotiating a scattering of avoidance areas and noise-sensitive spots (farms, hospitals, etc.). Low-level flying is thus illustrated as being very demanding, having to cope with restricted airspace, bird hazards, other aircraft, bad weather, and still maintain 250ft, while following a pre-determined route, keeping an eye on fuel, talking to air traffic controllers and, in many cases, leading a formation of other Hawks too. To the untrained observer it looks very easy, despite sounding like an impossible task. In reality it is an impossible task, at least for a new student.

The next ground feature to look for is a steep hillside on the western edge of Lake Vyrnwy, which serves to confirm that we are still on track. This time, thanks to some warning from my instructor, I manage to see the spot we are looking for, as it seemingly thunders by us at 420 knots, almost within touching distance, or so it seems. Racing onwards, literally bouncing in the turbulence, we approach our IP, our Initial Point which serves as a 'funnel feature' into a representative target run. Replacing the 1:500,000 scale map with a larger 1:50,000 chart, we arrive at our IP, which is a spot height on the A543 road at Bryn Trillyn, south-west of Denbigh. By looking at the larger map one can identify key features

which lead the eye towards the selected target, in this case a small bridge on the River Elwy, south of Abergele. The map has already been marked with ten-second intervals for me, but despite a running commentary from the front seat, I find it impossible to read the map accurately and simultaneously indentify the real features outside the cockpit at such phenomenal speed. I choose to look directly for the target, and with some

Left: Canopy open, the student prepares to climb into the Tucano for a solo sortie.

Right: Last-minute details are noted on the student's knee-pad before heading for the flightline.

Right: Busy scene at the Operations Desk.

verbal assistance I manage to find it, even though we are virtually overhead by the time I realize where we are. My instructor assures me that the skill can be developed, in time.

Having visually 'attacked' our target, we make a steep climb out of the bumpy low-level airspace, and head for the crisp blue sky above us, in order to see some other aspects of the Hawk's capability. First of all, an opportunity to sample the Hawk's uncomplicated stalling characteristics, and with a climb rate in excess of 4,000ft per minute, we quickly reach an altitude of 10,000ft, where we make a careful 360-degree search of the surrounding airspace, before starting the demonstration. The throttle is pulled back, and the airspeed slowly bleeds away as our attitude becomes distinctly nose-high. A gentle wing buffet signifies that we are approaching the stall, and suddenly we are descending. With a burst of power and the control column placed centrally forward, the recovery is swift, and the whole manoeuvre is distinctly unexciting. Back in the early days of the Hawk's developmental flying, the aircraft did posess rather less pleasant stalling characteristics, hence the addition of airflow breaker strips along the Hawk's wing leading edge, which provided a more satisfactory stall warning, and wing fences, which cured a fairly severe wing-drop problem.

Stalling complete, we return to our nominal height of 10,000ft, where the instructor invites me to take the controls. As I am distinctly in the non-pilot category, the opportunity to 'play' with an aircraft in the Hawk's category is something of a rare treat, although one's initial reaction is, perhaps naturally, to be over-cautious with the controls. It quickly becomes clear that only the smallest of movements on the control column is needed to achieve fairly large pitch and roll changes. After some encouragement from the front cockpit, I begin to gain some confidence and try my hand at snap rolls to port and starboard. At first, the overwhelming urge is to close one's eyes, but the gut-churning and totally disorientating effect of high speed rolls quickly becomes enjoyable, almost addictive. The instructors are keen to point out that in many respects the Hawk's handling characteristics are very similar to the Tucano's, just a little faster. Likewise, the Tornado is often referred to (at least in terms of handling) as a 'big Hawk'. To sample something of the Hawk's turning capability, I am instructed to put the aircraft into a left-hand turn, and with some care I achieve a fairly steady 3g turn. The instructor invites me to pull back on the

Left: The pre-flight briefing, and the student talks his way through the planned sortie, with the aid of an overhead projector, while the instructor listens and questions.

Below left: Hard at work, the student draws-up the map for his next navigational sortie.

Right: The relaxed atmosphere of the crewroom where the students and instructors can take a break between sorties.

Below: Long hours of academic toil during Ground School.

The Training

Left: The Ops Desk, as three instructors note some pre-flight details. The day's Notams (Notices to Airmen) and Royal Flight routes are posted on the wall.

Right: The briefing, where a formation sortie is being detailed by a QFI.

Right: The QFI takes a last glance at the sortie details before heading out to the flightline.

Far right: Busy scene as the instructors complete paperwork, prepare projection slides, and update flight information.

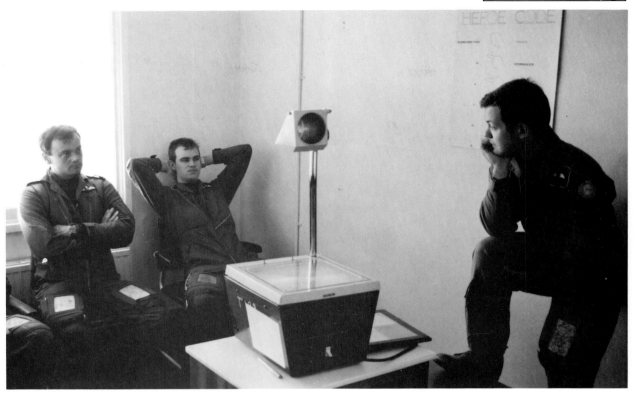

Left: Royal Flights, as visible on the wall, are always posted at the Ops Desk, as all RAF activity must be kept well clear of the planned Royal/VIP flights. Other day-to-day restrictions, avoidance areas and other updates are also posted on the board.

stick still further, through 4g, and 5g, my g-suit fiercely gripping my legs and stomach as I sink heavily into my seat. My instinct is to ease off, but I hear 'a little more, a little more', and we're at 6g, and still we're turning. The Hawk is stressed to 8g, and 6g is a day-to-day maximum regularly achieved by students. It is a pretty severe amount, and, in just a few seconds of sustained turning, can lead to loss of vision, even blackout. Consequently, students like to build-up a 'g-tolerance'.

With this complete, it is time to return to Valley, and as we fly through the Menai 'gate', we head for RAF Mona, to sample a demonstration forced landing. Simulated engine failures are a regular part of the Tucano and Hawk training schedules, and as we approach the overhead at 5,000ft, the instructor calls the tower and declares a 'practice pan', cutting power and turning to starboard over the upwind end of the runway at the 'High Key' position. Speed slows to 165 knots, and we enter a descending turn through 4,500ft, heading downwind as the gear is extended. Arriving at the 'Low Key' point directly abeam the touch-down point, we're at 3,000ft, still turning and descending, the speed reducing to 150 knots. The flaps are extended, and as the runway slips into our 12 o'clock position, the instructor keeps the Hawk directed at the initial aiming point, roughly a third of the way down the runway. Once satisfied that we're going to reach the runway, the nose is repositioned towards the runway threshold, and we head steeply down, in a most alarming fashion, the ground seemingly

rushing up to meet us. Shortly before touch-down we flare-out the descent, and gently touch down on Mona's runway 23, rolling for a few hundred feet before selecting full power, unsticking, and climbing straight ahead, tucking away the gear and flaps.

Turning right, we stabilize at 1,000ft and 360 knots, as Valley's controllers give us permission to join the airfield circuit and land. Descending once again to 500ft we flash in over the airfield boundary, and break hard left in a 4g turn, climbing back to 1,000ft, extending the airbrake, and positioning on to the downwind leg. Speed reduces to 150 knots, and the gear is extended once more, with mid-flap selected. Once abeam the touch-down point (the runway threshold), we make a 180-degree decending turn on to finals, while lowering the flaps to the fully extended position. The aircraft is positioned on short final approach to runway 19, at 250ft and 130 knots, gently descending, and touching down at 115 knots. With a fairly stiff breeze almost directly on our nose, the landing run is short, and in a matter of minutes the aircraft is back on the flight line, as I reposition the canopy and seat safety-pins in their 'safe' locations. I also detach the leg restraints and, more importantly, the PSP connection. It is easy to forget about the PSP, but climbing out of an ejection seat with the connection still in place causes the automatic functioning of a distress beacon which will needlessly (and very embarrassingly) attract the attention of the nearby Search and Rescue Wessex helicopter

Right: Obviously a good day, as the smiling student watches his QFI complete some more pre-flight paperwork.

crews! It would also cost the culprit more than a few drinks in the Mess bar that night!

Once the engine has stopped, the canopy is opened and the remaining seat and PSP connections can be unfastened, the helmet removed, and I climb out of the cockpit, on to the port engine intake, and down the access ladder. For a passenger the flight is over, but for a student a detailed de-briefing would follow, tracing every aspect of the sortie, examining what, if anything, went wrong, and what can be improved and built-upon during the next sortie. For the aircraft the day certainly wasn't over, and an hour later XX184 was back in the air with another crew.

Just a brief taste of Hawk flying is sufficient to indicate that the advanced and tactical flying training syllabus is more than a little challenging. As the instructor says, 'The student has got to be able to do virtually anything at anytime. If we can't generate that ability to think and act flexibly at this stage in their training, then we're wasting our time.' The instructors are able to spot a number of potential faults as they begin to arise, thanks to their collective years of experience. Sometimes it can be a basic handling problem, perhaps being unable physically to control the aircraft properly in close formation. Sometimes it can be fuel awareness that proves the student's downfall. If he doesn't continually monitor the fuel situation he may not notice if he begins to use fuel faster than planned. He has to make sure that he can 'get home' with sufficient fuel, so he should make an effort to do something if the

problem arises, such as truncating part of a navigational route, or climbing out of a low-level route earlier than planned. Or maybe diverting to another airfield, as even that would mean that the student is at least aware of his fuel state, and has made a positive move to do something about it.

Poor navigation is another important point that the instructors watch out for, as is low flying — that is, flying too low, below the minimum 250ft. Sitting at 250ft, letting the hills rise and fall away beneath him, is just not acceptable. The student is expected to maintain 250ft at all times. Navigational faults often stem from a tendency to over-read the map. The key to successful visual navigation is, as the instructors explain, to be able to put the map down and not look at it. For example, if there is a leg of perhaps eight minutes to fly, in a straight line, the student is guaranteed to arrive at the end of the leg at a prescribed time, provided that he fly the speed accurately, and there is no significant crosswind. Consequently, the instructor will encourage the student to perform a work cycle, putting the map down, maybe for four minutes, then re-checking his position before continuing, or making speed or directional adjustments as necessary. The important point is to convince the student that putting the map down is not a recipe for disaster, and that he can look out for other aircraft, check fuel, and generally be more aware of what is going on. As one instructor points out, 'over-reading maps is a common fault, and it's rather like driving down a motorway, wanting to leave at exit twenty, and then checking his map against every exit until he gets there'. On the other hand, he also points out that the Hawk flies much faster than the average car travels down a motorway, and the kind of navigational error that can be achieved in a car in maybe an hour can be achieved in a Hawk in roughly seven minutes.

As the course progresses towards tactical weapons operations, the learning curve increases rapidly, and life gets even more difficult. The fear of failure is intense, but by this stage the students can at least be fairly confident that, if they do fail, they can probably re-role on multi-engine aircraft or helicopters. Indeed, some pilots go on to multi-engine types only to re-train later as fast-jet pilots, so the change in type doesn't have to be irreversible.

Having mastered the skills necessary to fly the Hawk safely and accurately, the student is now taught how to apply his capabilities by operating the Hawk as a weapons platform. Until 1992, the tactical weapons training course was totally separate from the advanced flying training syllabus, and was conducted at RAF Brawdy and Chivenor, within Strike Command. Now the advanced and weapons courses are combined, split between two identical Flying Training Schools at Valley and Chivenor. The aim, as an instructor explains, is, 'to take an *ab initio* student—abbos, we call 'em, and turn them into baby fighter pilots'. The Hawks utilized for weaponry instruction are fully combat capable, able to carry Sidewinder air-to-air missiles under each wing. The Hawks also wear the markings of four reserve air defence squadrons, and in the event of an armed conflict these Hawks would form part of the United Kingdom's air defence, being flown by FTS instructors.

One of the first tastes of tactical operations is flying in 'Battle Formation', a phrase which becomes familiar from here onwards, through the Operational Conversion Unit and on to an operational squadron. No longer does a formation consist of 'hanging on to the leader's wingtip'. The students now begin to separate their aircraft by lateral distances of maybe a mile or more. The first real introduction to weapons operations is what is called a 'Simple Cine' sortie, and is explained by a QFI: 'Many of the Hawks are fitted with gunsights, and likewise we also carry a cine camera which will film whatever is seen through that gunsight. We fly a dual sortie with an instructor and a solo sortie, following another Hawk, giving the student a chance to get used to the idea of aiming his gunsight at another aircraft.

We then develop the skills into Cine Weave sorties, during which the aircraft being chased starts to manoeuvre more severely, making the task of training the gunsight on to him that much more difficult. At this stage they're obviously not firing any bullets, but they are shooting a roll of film, and after these flights their accuracy will be assessed.'

Navigational skills are also developed, and by this stage the student will fly almost every sortie at a speed of 420 knots, making regular IP-to-target runs, formation flights, and many solo sorties, some of which will still be observed by a QFI or QWI (Qualified Weapons Instructor), who will 'chase' the student in a second aircraft. By way of an illustration of how a tactical sortie is flown, the author joined a two-aircraft exercise at RAF Chivenor, a low-level sortie around Wales, in a defensive battle formation. The meteorological brief indicated that the conditions would be less than perfect for flying, with broken cloud at a base of 1,500ft and a visibility of about 30km, although over north Cornwall there would be heavy sleet and hail showers.

I would take the back seat of XX186 while a QFI would fly from the front seat, acting as a wingman to a student pilot who would lead us around a route which he had planned. The student's back seat would also be occupied by a Staff Navigator, and this would be the first time that he had flown with anyone other than a QFI, effectively being the student's very first experience of flying with a navigator behind him, as he would on a front-line squadron. As indicated by the met brief, this would be quite a demanding sortie for the student, as he would be expected to adhere to his planned route as closely as possible, while navigating around the anticipated bad weather, back on to track. As I am regularly reminded, the clouds over Wales tend to have very solid centres. Our route is intended to take us north from Chivenor, across the Bristol Channel, into Wales, and on into two IP-to-target runs. The student was given the locations of the two targets, and plenty of advice as to how to plan a suitable route, but otherwise everything was left entirely up to him. There are no pre-set routes as such, and the complete exercise, from brief to debrief, would be under the direction of the student.

Strapping in, and pre-start checks are performed as normal, and at 11.40 the two Hawks, callsigns 'Kelly One' and 'Kelly Two' are on the threshold of Chivenor's runway 28, ready for a formation take-off in line-abreast formation. With XX352 on our starboard side, the throttles go

Right: Mission planning, as two instructors scrutinise maps of the local area, at Linton-on-Ouse.

Right: Happy faces all round as instructors and students prepare to leave for a formation sortie.

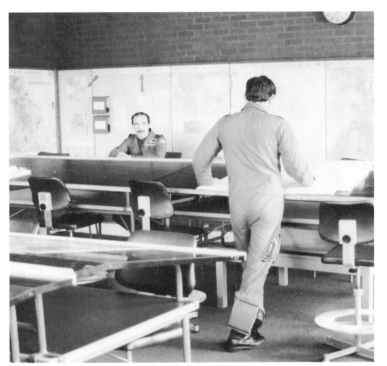

forward and, with a nod from the leader, the two aircraft surge forward, and twelve seconds later we are airborne, climbing straight ahead over the Devon coastline before turning right on to 030 degrees to take us north over the Bristol Channel, at 250ft. Once out over the expanse of grey water, we assume our tactical formation position, line-abreast, separated by roughly 2,000 yards. Over the featureless water it is easy to keep visual contact with the lead Hawk, although at times the separation does vary, and the aircraft becomes little more than a distant black shape low on the horizon. Speed increases to 420 knots, which equates to seven miles per minute, an acceptable speed for fuel economy, requiring about 93–94% power setting on the throttle. It would be possible to fly at 450 knots, but this would necessitate full power almost continually to maintain that speed at low level, whereas 420 knots is a more comfortable cruising speed which can easily be maintained.

Approaching the sprawling industrial complexes around Port Talbot, we pass over Mumbles Head, turning due north in a 'shackle' manoeuvre, a high-speed tactical turn, in which the lead

Left: The QFI in thoughtful mood as he prepares a low-level map of the local area.

aircraft (on our starboard side) passes across our 6 o'clock position, as we turn left, stabilizing on our port side. Re-acquiring our sister aircraft was difficult, at least to my untrained eye, despite having climbed to 2,000ft while crossing the Port Talbot area. Back at 250ft visual tracking is even more challenging. Another minute passes and the g-force winds on again, in a tight 5g shackle turn on to 305 degrees, making a three-minute run towards our first IP (Initial Point). My attention is constantly shifting between my attempts to keep track of the lead aircraft and my map, on which the QFI had drawn out the route. Over the IP, the student switches to his 1:50,000 scale Ordnance Survey map, as we race over a small estuary linking Camarthen with the Bay. Just to our left is the Pembrey weapons range, which is used by both 4FTS and 7FTS for air-to-ground attack profiles. Our target is a radio mast close to the A478 road, but I never even see it, being mentally lost in a confusion of rolling landscape, cloud, rain and g-force. We turn on to 096 degrees just a few miles east of RAF Brawdy, formerly the home of Chivenor's sister Tactical Weapons Unit.

Another tight turn on to 096 degrees takes us east on a five-minute run towards Llandovery, the weather gradually deteriorating, with increasing heavy showers forcing the student to lead us

around the worst patches, without straying too far from the intended route. His capacity to quick-think course corrections is vital, and, to complicate matters still further, other low-level aircraft are occasionally seen flashing between the hills in the charcoal grey murk. The seemingly open countryside can be surprisingly crowded at times. We turn hard on to 056 degrees through a long valley feature, with a patch of woodland appearing on the north-eastern side, as predicted by the map. A large hill with two aerial masts is our next turning-point, where we make another 5g turn on to 327 degrees towards our second Initial Point, through another valley, being careful to maintain a respectable separation from a nearby hospital. The target is located in a small village, within a 'basin feature' on the map, and at 420 knots we race overhead, before making another gut-wrenching 5g turn on to 218 degrees.

With the two targets successfully located, our route now takes us back towards Chivenor, still at low level, and to check whether the student is paying careful attention to his wingman, the QFI in the front seat of my aircraft decides to sneak in slowly towards the lead's 6 o'clock position. Not surprisingly, we didn't get too far before the student noticed our deliberate error, and requested us to move out of port again. Also very much on his mind at this stage is the amount of fuel remaining, and at various points in each sortie 'Bingo' fuel calls are made, denoting specific minimum amounts of remaining fuel to reach diversion airfields or home base. The Hawk's excellent range encourages any pilot to ignore the fuel status to some degree, but many combat aircraft are much less forgiving in terms of available fuel, so the QFIs try to teach the students healthy habits.

The final route turning-point rolls into view, in this case a spot height west of Lampeter, where we set course for the Bristol Channel on 183 degrees, turning on to 177 degrees as we cross the Welsh coastline, and close up our formation. Back at a more intimate distance from XX352, our respective speeds become much more evident, as the aircraft lurch up and down, left and right, in the turbulent low-level air. Earlier in the BFTS course, maintaining close formation would have been a major challenge for any student, whereas by now, on the way back to Chivenor, formation flying is almost taken for granted. We pull-up steeply to cross the coastline again near Ilfra-combe, and head for the airfield circuit at 500ft, reducing our speed to 360 knots. Sweat-soaked and exhausted, we're soon back on the ground for a detailed de-brief.

The course continues with more weaponry training, introducing the Strafe Phase, in which the student fires the Hawk's 30mm cannon (housed in an under-fuselage pod) at ground targets on the Pembrey range, near Swansea. Four sorties are flown, starting with a dual flight (with a QWI). When the student is adjudged to be safe, he flies a cine sortie, substituting film for bullets, and this will establish whether he can be trusted to fire live ammunition safely. He will then fly two more sorties using fifty rounds on each, flown against acoustic recording targets at Pembrey. After completion the film will be examined by a QWI, and the score recorded at the range. If either the QWI or range safety officer are not happy with the results, the sortie is 'DNCO'd' (Duty Not Carried Out), and is then re-flown, emphasizing that, even when flying solo, the student is still being constantly monitored.

Later in the syllabus the student is introduced to ACM (Air Combat Manoeuvring) the basic skills of the fighter pilot. Students are given a taste of ACM at RAF Coningsby, a front-line Tornado F3 base, and also the home of the RAF's Air Combat Simulator, a twin-dome computerized facsimile of the view from two Tornado F3 cockpits, in which the students can fight an opponent realisti-cally without leaving the ground. Coningsby's

simulator is quite convincing, and from the pilot's seat inside a representative Tornado cockpit the projected 360-degree picture surrounding the cockpit gives a good impression of actually being in the air. The simulated image of a marauding fighter is also most effective, and perhaps the only limiting factor is the fixed altitude of the projected image, which can lead the unwary to concentrate on the outside image, forget the altimeter, and crash.

The simulator gives students a 'feel' for the necessary skills, before taking to the air in their Hawks to fly ACM for real. At this stage, aerial combat is completely new to them, and although they have flown tail-chases, the concept of fighting another aircraft while trying not to get shot down, is both confusing and exciting. Initially the student flies roughly 300–500 yards behind a target aircraft, and uses the gun camera to simulate firing rounds of ammunition at the target Hawk. Dual sorties with a QWI are first flown, and then the student flies solo against an instructor. The emphasis then changes back to air-to-ground operations, flying more sorties over the Pembrey range, this time with practice bombs, progressing to a combined bombing and strafe configuration in which the student makes attacks with both bombs and ammunition on the same sortie. Once their ground-attack skills have been properly learned, the students then fly SAPs, (Simulated Attack Profiles), combining the navi-gation sorties with ground-attack profiles, flying simulated attacks against off-range targets. The sorties are planned, briefed and flown in their entirety by the students, and by this stage the available time to plan a sortie is also limited, with specific TOTs (Time Over Target) being given. In an operational environment, targets must be attacked at precise times, in order to coincide with attacks being flown by other RAF or NATO aircraft: 'there could be A-10s running in a couple of minutes ahead of you, and maybe a reconnais-sance Phantom a minute later, so timing is vital'. The instructors throw in a 'bounce' aircraft too, to add even more pressure. The 'bounce' is an additional Hawk flown by an instructor, simulat-ing an enemy fighter, attempting to break up and destroy the SAP formation.

Returning to air-to-air combat, live cannon firing is performed against a banner, towed by one of the unit's Hawks. The banner is basically a huge hessian flag, towed 800ft behind the Hawk, and dropped over the airfield after the sortie, enabling the instructors and students to see precisely how well, or how badly, they have fared. The bullets are painted with a coloured dye, which marks the target as the ammunition passes through. This allows up to six different aircraft to use the same target on one sortie. Simulated Sidewinder missile fits are also flown, using both the AIM-9G, a stern-attack weapon, and the AIM-9L, an all-aspect missile which can be launched at any angle from the target. Practice intercepts are introduced, and Combat Air Patrols (CAPs), during which the students will fly a racetrack pattern while awaiting direction towards incoming 'enemy' aircraft. As the Hawks do not have internal radar, there is obviously a limit to the amount of training that can be given in these particular aspects of air defence, but the course does provide a good grounding for further training at the Operational Conversion Unit. Safety is paramount throughout the course, and for ACM training a minimum base height of 10,000ft is always used, ensuring that the aircraft are always at least two miles above the ground. There also has to be absolutely no risk that the student is likely to collide with another aircraft.

As for the aircraft, the Hawk makes an excellent weapons trainer, and is recognized as being a very 'forgiving' machine. The students can mishandle the aircraft quite severely and it will still fly: 'it doesn't bite you', as one student comments. The Hawk is certainly an excellent trainer for the Tornado and European Fighter Aircraft, which also incorporate many 'foolproof' handling qualities. The only obvious potential problem is engine surge, which can be caused by flying in a heavy buffet, turning directly behind another aircraft, and any other way in which the airflow to the engine is likely to be disrupted. With too much fuel reaching the engine, and not enough air, it will surge, resulting in banging or loud popping, with a marked increase in gas turbine temperature. Normally, a swift closing of the throttle will cure the problem, but if the surge isn't caught quickly the engine must be stop-cocked and re-lit. It doesn't happen very often either during training or on operational squadrons, but the students must be trained to deal with the situation.

For tactical training the Hawks are limited to 6.9g, and although 7g and more wouldn't damage the aircraft, such stress would use up airframe fatigue life rapidly. Negative-g limit is set at -3.5, but as the QFI comments; 'you would have to do some fairly exotic aerobatics to reach that kind of figure, and as we're more concerned with combat, we try to leave that kind of flying to Pitts Special stunt planes'. Chivenor and Valley are

well positioned for Hawk operations, with plenty of unrestricted airspace all around, allowing the pilots simply to select areas with the best weather, to conduct the flying exercises. For ACM, the students are not permitted to fly in or even near cloud, because although running away into a cloud bank might be considered a valid tactic in a real fight, during training it is discouraged. Another restriction is the need to fly over the sea, because of the cannon ammunition which is being expelled. For ground-attack profiles, all off-range targets are predetermined and approved by the QWIs and QFI and are normally bridges, TV masts, towers, that kind of thing, and certainly are never private houses. Although the targets may be pre-selected, the students are free to select their own routes to them.

At the end of the 4FTS or 7FTS syllabus, the successful students are posted to an Operational

Below: The Tucano systems simulator, basically a precise copy of the 'real thing', in the safety of the Ground School complex.

Above: On the flightline at Valley, student and instructor prepare to get airborne.

Conversion Unit (OCU) appropriate to the type of aircraft they have been earmarked to fly. The FTS staff join RAF staff officers at a Role Dispersal Meeting, where they attempt to match students with available OCU slots. The OCUs are: 16(R) Squadron (Lossiemouth) for Jaguars, 20(R) Squadron (Wittering) for Harriers, TTTE (Cottesmore) for Tornado GR.1s, 56(R) Squadron (Coningsby) for Tornado F3. Sometimes there are not enough students to fill the slots, and sometimes the opposite is true, but in either case the instructors have a fairly good idea of which type of aircraft the student will be most suited to. Most will want to go to the Harrier or Jaguar OCU, simply for the 'thrill factor' of flying a single-seat machine, and the demand for places on the European Fighter Aircraft OCU is likely to be very great. However, most will be posted to the Tornado GR1 or F3, simply because of the larger number of Tornado fighters and bombers that are in service, and despite personal preferences, no student is exactly heartbroken if he doesn't get the posting he ideally wants. Students will normally have to wait between eight and ten weeks before joining an OCU, and for those who wait longest, some refresher flying will be offered at the FTS. The instructors are keen to point out that they will do whatever they can to make the student well-equipped for the OCU. By this stage in a student's RAF career, the training costs have been phenomenal, and understandably, the RAF would not want to lose a student after spending in excess of three million pounds, unless he really couldn't tackle the job or was simply unsafe in the air.

The Terminology

Below: Up the steps to the Hawk's cockpit. The canopy MDC is visible, and the raised position of the instructor's seat is evident.

The Terminology

Taxiing

Learning to taxi the Tucano is a fairly simple process which is easily mastered. However, as with almost every aspect of military aircraft operations, there are pitfalls for the unwary student. Taxiing skills are not taught in isolation from other flying exercises, and the essential techniques will be acquired during early training sorties. Subsequently the instructor will demonstrate how to cope with specific situations as and when they arise. Although taxiing an aircraft is a relatively simple task, the effect of windflow on the fuselage, together with the use of differential braking and reverse thrust, may produce unfamiliar effects. Strong crosswinds will affect the directional control. Because of the Tucano's long fuselage and large fin, the aircraft tends to behave like a weathercock turning into the wind; for example, a strong crosswind from the left will encourage the Tucano's nose to swing left. Strong winds will also deflect control surfaces, causing them to bang against their stops, which could possibly damage them, so the control column should he held firmly into one corner, to prevent damage. Tailwinds may trigger an automatic stall warning, which can be cancelled by using the Stall Warning Isolating Switch.

Unlike some aircraft, and road vehicles, the Tucano is equipped with differential brakes. Each mainwheel brake caliper is operated individually by the respective toebrake. Equal foot pressure on the brakes will slow the aircraft in a straight line, whereas unequal toebrake pressure will cause the aircraft to turn in the direction of the more heavily braked wheel. But differential braking increases stress on the undercarriage components and carries the risk of damaging the tyres, and should therefore only be used when necessary. The Tucano has a small amount of available reverse thrust which varies in effectiveness depending upon engine RPM and airspeed, but even at low taxiing speeds and with the engine set at 70% RPM, it will offer some useful additional control. Reverse thrust should be used to slow the aircraft before wheel braking is applied, as necessary.

Taxyways are normally marked by a broken white line, painted down the centreline. These markings are only intended to denote the exact position of the centreline, and while it is generally good policy to follow the line in a small aircraft like the Tucano, the centreline markings take no account of the mainwheel track of larger aircraft, and consequently bigger aircraft could leave the taxyway on tight corners, by following the painted line. Additional markings are applied to the Aircraft Servicing Platform (ASP) to assist with positioning, and departure from these lines may reduce clearances from ground equipment. The captain of the aircraft is always responsible for the safety of his aircraft, and it is his responsibility to avoid collision with other aircraft and obstacles when taxiing, even when under the direction of a ground marshaller. If there is any doubt about adequate clearance from any obstacles, the captain should stop and request assistance. If there is still any doubt, the aircraft should be shut down, and towed to a less-restricted manoeuvring area. The Tucano's wings extend 17 feet on each side of the fuselage, and this should be borne in mind.

R/T clearance must be obtained from Air Traffic Control (ATC) before an aircraft is allowed to taxi. Taxiing aircraft have right of way over vehicles and pedestrians, but not over other towed aircraft. A good lookout is important before crossing a runway, and a runway should never be crossed before obtaining permission from ATC. The Tucano's engine is very powerful, and excessive use of power will produce rapid accelerations, additionally creating substantial propwash, which can cause damage to other aircraft, or endanger personnel. Taxiing speed should be limited to a fast walking pace in confined areas, on bends, at night and on wet/icy taxyways. On longer, straight sections in dry conditions it is safe to taxy at faster speeds, but it should be borne in mind that undue use of the wheel brakes will cause higher than normal brake disc and tyre temperatures, which may significantly increase the stopping distance required when aborting a take-off.

Effects of Controls

The Tucano is equipped with conventional aerodynamic controls. In the early stages of basic flying training it is convenient to assume that each control will work in only one axis, but in later sorties it will be demonstrated that both the rudder and aileron produce further effects. Four forces act on an aircraft in flight, these being: thrust, drag, lift and weight. In level and unaccelerated flight these forces are balanced, with weight and lift acting against each other, as do thrust and drag. However, the balance between these coupled forces will vary depending upon the centre of gravity, the amount of thrust and drag. Although the forces can be arranged to balance each other, there will normally be a residual imbalance, causing either a nose-up or nose-down pitching moment.

To keep the aircraft from pitching down, the pilot must pull back on the control column to obtain up-elevator, and the reverse also applies. Naturally a continual force applied on the stick will eventually become uncomfortable for the pilot to hold, so trimming devices are fitted which enable the pilot to select the desired elevator position without using the stick. The trim switch operates a small aerofoil tab which serves to 'fly' the elevator at the chosen deflection, thus avoiding the need to displace the control column. When the control forces in each axis are reduced to zero in this way, the aircraft is 'in trim'. The Tucano has trim tabs for all three axes. Aileron and elevator trim are driven by a single twin-axis switch on top of the control column, the rudder trim being operated by a switch on the forward face of the throttle.

Pushing the throttle forward increases the engine power, coarsening the pitch of the propeller and causing a corresponding increase in thrust. Changing thrust will upset the balance of forces acting on the aircraft, requiring it to be re-trimmed. Unlike a jet aircraft, power changes in the Tucano also produce changes in directional trim. The slipstream produced by the propeller rotates helically around the fuselage, eventually hitting the port face of the fin, producing a yawing

Above: Valley's flightline. A student and instructor approach their waiting Hawk trainer.

Above: Solo student taxies to the runway in XX184.

movement. As airspeed is increased, the helical flow elongates, thus striking the fin at a smaller angle, which reduces the yawing effect. Also at higher airspeed the fin becomes an increasingly effective stabilizer, which reduces the yawing tendency still further. Therefore the strongest yawing movements are produced when applying full power at low speed.

Lookout and 'Foeel'

Military pilots rely on the 'see and be seen' principle to avoid collisions in VMC (Visual Meterological Conditions). As most military aircraft are camouflaged, visual detection can be particularly difficult at times, and a thorough lookout is always essential, even when concentrating on other tasks. For ease of reporting, pilots use a clock code system to relay information about visual contacts, relating the contact's position to a relative location on a clock-face, assuming that straight ahead is 12 o'clock, 90 degrees to the right is 3 o'clock, and so on.

In addition to lookout, it is important regularly to monitor the position and condition of the aircraft. The appropriate checks are listed in the Tucano Flight Reference Cards carried on each flight by the student, and are known by a mnemonic, FOEEL. A FOEEL check should be carried out roughly every ten minutes:

■ **Fuel.** Check the contents remaining, and the fuel flow. This will establish how much longer the sortie can be flown before returning to base. Check fuel balance, and if an imbalance is noticeable, the fuel tanks are trimmed by selecting both fuel pumps to ON on the heavier side of the aircraft, and leaving one pump ON on the lighter side.

■ **Oxygen.** The student should check his oxygen contents, the two connections, the flow, and check that the instructor's oxygen indicator is still blinking.

■ **Engine.** Check that all indications are within limits.

■ **Electrics.** As specified.

■ **Location.** Should be fixed using visual features

if possible, or by using Tacan and a kneepad map. Care should be taken when using a kneepad map, as if only one minute is taken to fix location, the aircraft will have covered three miles without the pilot having looked out of the aircraft.

Straight and Level

The visual attitude required to fly straight and level at 180 knots remains constant. If the aircraft accelerates from 180 knots to 220 knots, keeping the visual attitude constant, the wing will produce more lift. The weight of the Tucano hasn't changed and so the aircraft will climb; in order to stay level, the aircraft's AOA must be reduced, to compensate. As the aircraft accelerates, the nose must be progressively lowered, and the reverse applies when decelerating. As IAS (Indicated Air Speed) increases, so does the effectiveness of the fin and rudder, and where relatively large rudder deflections are required to maintain a straight path at low speeds and high power, the rudder deflection should be reduced at higher speeds.

Turns

Newton stated that a body in a state of uniform motion, travelling in a straight line, will continue to do so until compelled to change by an applied force. So, to turn the aircraft, a force must be applied to it, this being lift. Of course, lift is a force which acts at right angles to the relative airflow, and increasing lift while flying straight and level will simply cause the aircraft to climb. To turn, the lift vector must be inclined, to enable some of it to act in the horizontal plane. However, if the lift vector is simply inclined, the vertical component would no longer be sufficient to maintain level flight, and the aircraft would descend. Therefore, the total lift must be increased, by increasing the angle of attack of the wing, i.e., moving the control column aft. So for a successful level turn, both bank and back pressure is required on the stick.

Fuel Economy

Since power is produced by burning fuel, it is fair to say that the slower the aircraft flies, the longer

Below: As a Hawk begins a take-off roll, a second Hawk prepares to line-up. The white numbers painted on the Hawk's nose and tail are a repeat of the last three digits of the aircraft serial number (just visible on the rear fuselage). The additional '2' on the tail signifies that this aircraft belongs to No 2 Squadron of 4FTS.

it can remain airborne. However, as a compromise between fuel economy and aircraft manoeuvrability, most training sorties are flown at 180 knots, which also equates to an easy-to-calculate three miles per minute. There are occasions when the aircraft has to be flown for endurance, for example, when asked to 'hold off' by ATC, while another aircraft or emergency is dealt with. In this case the aircraft speed should be reduced to 110–115 knots, minimizing throttle movements and flying as gently as possible, to reduce fuel consumption.

Effect of Landing Gear and Airbrake

Extending the flaps, airbrake or landing gear into the aircraft slipstream will cause additional lift and/or drag. This in turn will cause an immediate change in trim due to the changes in aerodynamic forces acting on the aircraft. The extra drag will then cause the aircraft to decelerate, again upsetting the balance of forces, causing a longer-term trim change. In practice, the operation of ancillary services is normally accompanied by an

intentional change in airspeed. For example, when the undercarriage is lowered downwind to land at 140 knots, the increase in drag is deliberately used to reduce airspeed to 115 knots. This change in IAS will change the overall trim, and so the transient out-of-trim forces are not trimmed-out, being held on the control column, and the longer-term change is then corrected by trimming when established at the revised airspeed. In short, the immediate effect of extending the airbrake is to cause a nose-up change in pitch (the opposite also applying). Extending the landing gear causes a nose-up and then a nose-down change, the reverse being the case when raising the undercarriage.

Effect of Flap

Lowering the flaps will alter both the lift and drag of the aircraft, which again will result in trim changes. Lowering MID flap produces a relatively large increase in lift for a relatively small drag penalty, and an accompanying nose-up change in pitch. Full flap (DOWN) will produce a large drag increase, a small increase in lift, and a nose-down pitch change. Because MID flap creates lift, the aircraft will climb if the pitch attitude is not modified. As the IAS subsequently reduces and lift decreases, the nose must then be raised to maintain level flight. Selecting flap in the Tucano will always increase lift, so a lower nose attitude will always be required for level flight with flap extended.

Climbing

In order to maintain a climb at any given IAS, more power must be provided than for the same IAS in level flight. While in level flight the thrust is only required to overcome drag, in a climb the thrust has to overcome the drag and lift the weight of the aircraft. The power necessary to overcome drag is referred to as 'Power Required', and the amount of power produced by the aircraft's propulsion system is known as the 'Power Available'. If the power available exceeds the power required the excess power can be used to climb the aircraft, and the greater the excess, the faster the rate of climb. In the Tucano the maximum excess power occurs close to the minimum drag speed, so the best rate of climb in the Tucano is achieved at speeds around 125 knots, i.e., relatively slow. Because the Tucano has a great deal of excess power, the aircraft would need to be flown at an AOA of about 15 degrees nose-up in order to take advantage of the best climb speed, climbing so steeply that the day-to-day training altitude would be reached while still in the airfield vicinity. Naturally general handling sorties are not flown close to the airfield, so there would be little point in making such a steep climb. Normal sorties will be flown at a climb-out speed of 170 knots, which will give a greater horizontal separation from the airfield, and, because of the lower nose attitude, will improve the student's forward visibility during the climb.

Descending

As explained, excess power will enable the aircraft to climb, the mechanical energy of the engine being converted to potential energy. If, for whatever reason, the power available becomes a smaller amount than the power required, the aircraft will naturally decelerate, so if the pilot wishes to maintain a given IAS he must convert potential energy to kinetic energy, by descending. It follows that the greater the deficit in energy, the faster potential energy has to be converted, requiring a higher rate of descent. So, for any given IAS and drag configuration, the power setting will dictate the rate of descent. A standard visual descent in the Tucano is flown at 180 knots, with the throttle set at FLT IDLE, and the airbrake in. This is a good compromise configuration, balancing the need to descend quickly and the need to make headway back to base.

FIRAC Checks

Before beginning any descent it is important to establish that the aircraft is properly prepared, and FIRAC checks are designed to cover the appropriate points, and should be carried out every time a recovery to any airfield is made, or before a descent to low level:

■ **Fuel.** Ensure that there is sufficient fuel for recovery to base. If there isn't enough fuel, this is the best time to find out, because the aircraft burns less fuel at altitude, and the recovery can be modified to save fuel, or a diversion to another airfield can be initiated.

■ **Instruments.** Just about every descent will involve the possibility of flying into cloud, so it is important that the student check that both attitude indicators are erect, and that the compass is erect and synchronized. Entering cloud with unreliable instruments is almost guaranteed to create a disaster.

■ **Radio.** The appropriate radio frequency for recovery should be set.

■ **Altimeters.** Unless a clearance down to a flight level is anticipated, both altimeters should be set to the QFE reading. Before descending, the two altimeters should be cross-checked to ensure that neither is giving an erroneous reading. If there is a discrepancy, the altimeter with the lowest reading should be used.

■ **Conditioning.** A rapid descent from the cold air at altitude to the warmer and moister air at lower levels will cause rapid misting of the canopy. After a prolonged period of flying at altitude, the

Above: Busy scene at Valley as a Hawk taxies to the runway, past just one of Valley's Hawk flightlines.

cockpit should be warmed before descending, to prevent misting.

Mis-setting or mis-reading of an altimeter, or failure to notice a mis-reading altimeter during descent, will greatly increase the possibility of colliding with the ground. Altimeters should be cross-checked at least every 5,000ft in descents that are above 10,000ft, and at least every 2,000ft at any lower altitudes. It is also considered good practice for students to call out the height to which he has been cleared every time the altimeter is checked. This will reduce the chances of inadvertently descending through the cleared height, and, as an additional safeguard, IMC (Instrument Met Conditions) descents below 2,000ft should be restricted to a maximum descent rate of 1,000ft per minute.

Climbing Turns

As previously explained, the rate of climb depends upon the amount of excess power available. The Tucano has a considerable amount of excess power which can be both a help or a hindrance. When climbing away from the airfield circuit, the reserves of excess power can be used to good effect, gaining height quickly. However, the climb is made to only 1,000ft in the circuit, and climbing at full power would generate a higher rate of climb than is necessary. Consequently, once the undercarriage and flaps have started to retract after take-off, the power is reduced to 60% Tq, which provides sufficient excess power to climb away safely and quickly. Because the downwind leg of the circuit is flown

at 140 knots (below the landing gear's limiting speed), the upwind turn is also made at this speed, and this combination of speed and power produces an unfamiliar climbing attitude, which the instructor will demonstrate to the student.

An ideal climbing turn in the airfield circuit will cover precisely 180 degrees in 500ft of climb. Temperature, wind and flying accuracy will affect this aim however, and sometimes the downwind heading will be reached before attaining 1,000ft, and conversely, 1,000ft is sometimes reached before the downwind heading. In the case of the latter situation, power can be used to make a smooth transition from a climbing turn to a level turn. Reducing torque to the point where available power equals the power required, and by lowering the nose, the aircraft can be levelled off, while still holding 45 degrees of bank. This level turn is then maintained until the downwind leg is reached.

Descent Techniques

Regardless of the aircraft configuration, there are two methods of controlling descent:
■ The aircraft attitude is used to maintain a constant airspeed, while the power is used to control the rate of descent (the flight path).
■ The attitude is used to fly the appropriate flight path, and the power is used to control the airspeed.

Both techniques can be and are used in the Tucano. The former method (attitude for airspeed) is normally used when there is no specific visual aiming-point for the descent (usually the finals turn), and most descents are flown using this technique. However the latter method (attitude for flight path) is used when there is a specific visual aiming-point for the descent, such as on a visual approach to the runway when landing. It is important to understand both techniques, and when each should be used.

As previously explained, if the power available is less than the power required, the aircraft must descend if the speed is to be maintained. Students

Left: Hawk duo taxiing on to the runway.
Formation sorties form a regular part of the 4FTS and 7FTS Hawk flying syllabus.

are initially taught to descend with the throttle set at FLT IDLE. Because closing the throttle reduces the power available to a minimum, a high rate of descent has to be flown in order to maintain the speed, but it is dangerous to fly such high rates of descent while in the airfield circuit, especially during the finals turn with landing gear and flaps down. At this stage the rate of descent is controlled with power, never by using the airbrake. With some power applied, less potential energy needs to be converted to kinetic energy, and a higher nose attitude will maintain the desired speed, thus decreasing the rate of descent. The rate of descent round the finals turn can be accurately controlled in this manner. By extending the flaps, undercarriage and airbrake, drag is increased, but the propeller also creates drag. At roughly 10% torque (Tq) the propeller will generate zero thrust. Below 10% the propeller will generate drag. Reducing Tq to below 10% can cause a rapid decrease in speed, if a constant attitude is held. Equally, a rapid increase in the rate of descent will be created if the speed is kept constant, and naturally neither situation is desirable when flying the finals turn at low speed in a high-drag configuration. The instructor will demonstrate the very high sink rates which can occur in this situation, emphasizing why it is so dangerous to throttle back to FLT IDLE on the finals turn.

Stalling–Clean Configuration

Lift is generated by a pressure differential of the airflow over the wing. This pressure differential will increase as the AOA of the wing is increased. The Tucano's wing is designed to operate over a range of angles of attack, roughly −4 degrees to +15 degrees, which is more than sufficient for typical training operations. However, as the AOA approaches 15 degrees, the point at which the airflow separates from the wing begins to move forward from the wing's trailing edge. Eventually, as the AOA is increased, the separated airflow will be felt through the control column as 'buffet', caused by the disrupted airflow passing over the tail surface. The airflow becomes increasingly separated, but still generates lift, until reaching a point at which lift begins to decrease, and this is the Stalling Angle. Increasing the AOA beyond this will cause most of the airflow to separate from the wing, causing a rapid loss of lift, and the aircraft starts to sink. Further increases in AOA will simply produce heavier buffet.

The Terminology

The transition between an attached airflow and the complete separation of airflow occurs within a very narrow band of AOA, as little as one degree. This is a significant factor, which affects the characteristics of each stall. Ideally, the Tucano's two wings would be perfectly identical in every respect, stalling at precisely the same angle as each other, causing the nose to drop with the wings remaining level, but manufacturing tolerances do not incorporate such precision, and so the wings are not completely identical and do not stall at precisely the same angle as each other. As one wing stalls before the other, the aircraft will roll towards the stalled wing, and naturally the roll could be in either direction. Attempting to correct the roll by using aileron inputs will only exacerbate the problem, as down aileron will increase the AOA of the stalled wing, further increasing the asymmetry in lift, and increasing the rate of roll. Consequently the wings should be unstalled before making any aileron inputs.

Stall Symptoms

Closing the throttle and maintaining straight and level flight will cause speed to decrease. This in itself is a warning that the stalling angle is approaching. As the speed decreases further the nose is raised progressively in order to maintain level flight. The AOA will increase steadily, and as the speed reduces, the controls will begin to feel less effective. Finally, the audio stall warning device will sound, and shortly afterwards light buffet will be felt through the control column. The basic symptoms of an approaching stall, therefore, are:
- A low speed which is still reducing.
- A high nose attitude.
- An increasing angle of attack.
- Decreasing control effectiveness.
- Audio stall warning.
- Light buffet felt through the control column.

If all these warnings are ignored and an attempt is made to hold level flight, the aircraft will enter a full stall. The first indication will be the increase in light buffet to a more pronounced heavy buffet, felt through the whole airframe. At the stall the nose will drop and the aircraft will sink, possibly rolling left or right, while the audio stall warning continues to sound. The symptoms of a full stall, therefore, are:
- Heavy buffet felt through the airframe and controls.
- Nose drop.

- Sink.
- Possible wing drop in either direction.
- Audio warning sound in the cockpit.

During the BFTS course the Tucano is deliberately stalled in order to practise the stall recovery procedure. All stall recoveries are made on the assumption of a worst-case scenario, where the aircraft is close to the ground. The aim, therefore, is to recover from the stall with the minimum of height loss, as there is little point in successfully unstalling an aircraft if it crashes into the ground during the procedure. Without doubt the safest recovery is one made before the onset of a full stall. The first priority of a recovery is to reduce the AOA. Moving the control column forward will stop the buffeting, reducing the AOA below the stalling angle. If there is wing drop, it will immediately reduce, and having successfully unstalled the wings, the next priority is to increase the airspeed so as to avoid re-entering the stall.

Above: Both crew members safely attached to their ejection seats, and the canopy is pulled down ready to close.

Lowering the nose will trade height for speed, or alternatively an increase in power will cause the aircraft to accelerate. The second action, therefore, is to apply full power; to save time and height loss the power is simultaneously applied as the stick is moved forward. In order to ensure that all of the available lift can be used effectively, the wings are levelled, and as the aircraft accelerates the nose is raised to ease out of the descent. It is important to remember that there will be some powerful and continually changing trim forces during the stall recovery. Finally, full power checks should be made when safely established in a climb. Collectively these actions are known as the Standard Stall Recovery, summarized as:

■ Control column is held centrally forward until buffet stops.
■ Apply full power simultaneously with stick input.
■ Level the wings.

■ Ease out from the descent.
■ Trim the aircraft.
■ Complete full power checks when established in a climb.

Should the stall be approached inadvertently at any time, there is no point in waiting for all stall symptoms to appear, and at the onset of any of the described symptoms the stall recovery action should be initiated.

HASSELL Checks

Before manoeuvring the Tucano in all three planes, or before any exercises that will involve reduced manoeuvrability or a temporary loss of control, essential checks must be carried out. These checks will ensure that, whenever such manoeuvres are flown, they are made in a fully serviceable aircraft which is correctly configured, and that the aircraft is in clear airspace with

The Terminology

Below: XX203, wearing the markings of No 63 Squadron, one of the former Tactical Weapons Unit 'Shadow' squadrons at Chivenor.

The Terminology

sufficient recovery height in case something should go wrong. These checks are collectively known by the mnemonic (HASELL) and are:

■ **Height.** There must be sufficient height to recover before reaching 5,000ft when flying duel, or 8,000ft when flying solo. The aircraft must also be at least 3,000ft from any cloud. For stalling exercises, 2,000ft above the minimum height should be sufficient for safe recovery.

■ **Airframe.** The flaps and landing gear should be in the appropriate position for the manoeuvre, and for a clean configuration stall they should both be selected UP. The airbrake should be tested as it may be required.

■ **Security.** Check that the harness is both tight and locked. All loose articles should be stowed. Map bin lids should be secured, pockets should be fastened, and a check should be made that there are no pens stowed unfastened in the external holders on the flying suit.

Right: The 7FTS flightline at Chivenor in Devon. The grey/green disruptive camouflage visible on the distant aircraft is now completely replaced by 'air defence grey'.

Below: The pre-flight walk-round check.

Left: Instructor and student walking out to their Hawk on Valley's blustery flightline.

Right: The student receives some kind assistance from the ground crew as he straps into his ejection seat.

Left: Short finals to land, the student obviously working hard as he leans forward in his seat. The instructor keeps a careful watch from his lofty position.

■ **Engine.** The RPM, EGT oil pressure and temperature must all be within acceptable limits. Check that there is sufficient fuel, and that the fuel contents do not fall outside the balance limits for the aircraft.

■ **Location.** Fix the aircraft position by using radio aids, or by a visual check. Ensure that the aircraft is clear of any active airfields, built-up areas or controlled airspace.

■ **Lookout.** Ensure that the aircraft is clear of cloud by at least 3,000ft vertically, and that there are no other aircraft in the vicinity.

Stalling–Approach Configuration

Having learned to recover the Tucano from an incipient and fully developed stall with landing gear and flaps selected UP, the next stage is to achieve the same capability with the aircraft set up in the approach configuration, with landing gear and flaps selected DOWN. The instructor will demonstrate to the student what will happen if the Tucano stalls fully in the finals turn, and the rapid roll and height loss should convince the student that the symptoms of an inadvertent approaching stall should not be ignored under any circumstances. Recovery should be made upon recognition of the first symptom. There are five major factors that affect a stall:

■ **Weight.** More lift will be needed to maintain level flight, if extra weight is carried. Consequently a higher airspeed will be required at any AOA, including the stalling angle, and therefore, the weight of the aircraft will increase the basic stalling speed.

■ **Flaps.** At a given AOA the flaps will increase the lift which is generated by the wings, and so the speed necessary to maintain level flight will

Left: All aboard, as the student climbs into his cockpit.

be reduced, thus lowering the stalling speed. Extended flaps will also increase the airframe buffet which could mask the less-severe pre-stall buffet, and the slight asymmetry of extended flaps will increase the likelihood of wing drop at the stall.

■ **Thrust.** If the aircraft should stall with power applied, the line of thrust will be inclined upwards as the AOA increases, and a component of the thrust will act vertically upwards, supporting some of the aircraft weight. The propwash flowing over the wings may also cause some increase in lift, and the combined effect is to cause the aircraft to stall at a lower speed. The reduction in effective AOA over the wing's inboard section also means that the stall will occur at a higher nose-up angle.

■ **Icing and Airframe Damage.** Damage to the aerofoils, or accumulations of ice, may cause an increase in the stalling speed, by altering the effective cross-section of the aerofoil, thus reducing its lifting characteristics, or causing an early disruption of the airflow over the wing. Of course there will also be an increase in the aircraft weight in the case of icing accumulations.

■ **Loading.** All manoeuvres, apart from a pure roll, will require a centripetal force, provided by increasing the load factor, and having exactly the same effect as increasing the weight of the aircraft. The stalling speed will therefore increase when 'g' is applied.

As only a small margin exists between the onset of buffet and a fully developed stall in the Tucano, particularly with gear and flaps extended, two independent artificial stall warning systems are incorporated into the aircraft. An AOA vane provides information for an AOA gauge, AOA indexer and the AOA audio warning. Additionally, the stall warning vane provides information for the stick shaker facility, and both the audio warning and stick shaker operate roughly four to six knots above the stalling speed. It should be remembered that the stick shaker only operates when the gear and flaps are down. If the AOA and stall vane heaters are not switched on, or if they fail, the systems may fail in icing conditions. Consequently it is important to switch on the AOA/STALL heaters after take-off.

Circuits

Air Traffic Control is responsible for the control of all aircraft movements on the airfield and in the

Right: A last-minute word with the groundcrew before climbing into the cockpit. Note the QFI's fire-retardant gloves.

Right: Engine running, XX184 is ready to taxy out from the flightline, aided by the ground marshaller.

The Terminology

Below: Flaring for touchdown, this 4FTS Hawk displays the blue-topped fuselage, part of an on-going variation in colour schemes, aimed at achieving the most highly-visible anti-collision combination of colours. Unlike front-line RAF aircraft, training aircraft need to be seen to be safe.

airfield circuit area. Within the airfield's Military Air Traffic Zone (MATZ), all ATC instructions are mandatory and must be obeyed, unless the aircraft captain considers that the action would endager the aircraft. Local ATC is normally divided between air operations and ground operations, each with an individual radio frequency and controller. The engine start and taxi will be the responsibility of a ground controller, whereas take-off, landing and circuit flying will be under a local controller. The circuit is divided into three sectors: the upwind leg; the downwind leg; the finals turn and finals approach.

Allocation of Landing Priority

It is important to make R/T calls when in the correct geographical position, since the order of landing priority is made according to the reported position rather than by the physical position in the airfield circuit. An aircraft that has called 'finals' will have priority over an aircraft still flying downwind. Likewise an aircraft calling 'downwind' has priority over aircraft upwind. If there is more than one aircraft in any sector, the one which calls first is assumed to be in front and has priority. At a BFTS, an aircraft making an instru-

ment approach reaches what is the equivalent of finals at three miles from touch-down. As the aircraft will be controlled on a separate frequency, the final clearance to land will not be heard by other aircraft in the circuit, therefore details will be relayed by the local controller.

Terminology

■ **Go-Around.** Discontinuing a circuit at any stage is referred to as a 'go-around', and although a final approach can still be made, no attempt should be made to either land or roll down the runway. The go-around should be initiated at 200ft or more. Continuing to make an approach below this height will cause the runway caravan controller to fire a red Very flare. 'Overshoot' has the same meaning.

■ **Overshoot/Undershoot.** The former describes an approach that would end in a landing beyond the designated touch-down point. The latter refers to a landing that would occur before the touch-down point.

■ **Roller Landing.** Describes a landing that is immediately followed by another take-off, without stopping on the runway. Speed does not normally fall below 10–15 knots of the rotating

Below: Strapping-in; a relatively simple process in the Hawk. No, the 'VAL' is not a name, it is the three-letter code for Valley.

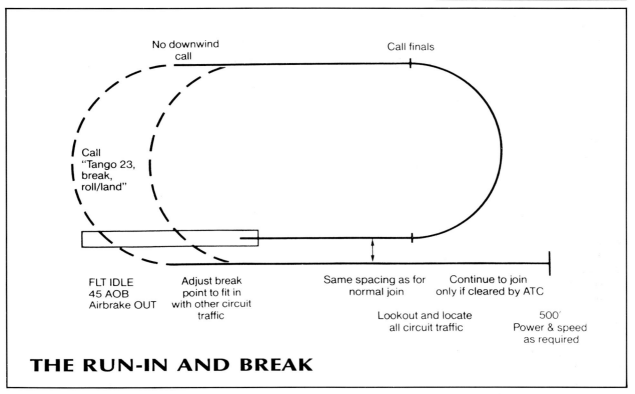

No downwind call

Call finals

Call "Tango 23, break, roll/land"

FLT IDLE
45 AOB
Airbrake OUT

Adjust break point to fit in with other circuit traffic

Same spacing as for normal join

Continue to join only if cleared by ATC

Lookout and locate all circuit traffic

500'
Power & speed as required

THE RUN-IN AND BREAK

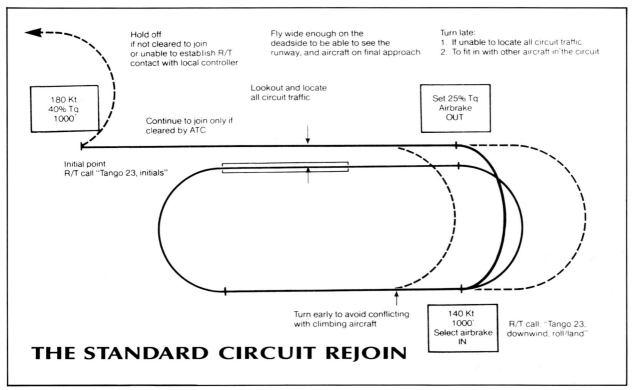

Hold off
if not cleared to join or unable to establish R/T contact with local controller

Fly wide enough on the deadside to be able to see the runway, and aircraft on final approach

Turn late:
1. If unable to locate all circuit traffic
2. To fit in with other aircraft in the circuit

180 Kt
40% Tq
1000'

Lookout and locate all circuit traffic

Set 25% Tq
Airbrake
OUT

Continue to join only if cleared by ATC

Initial point
R/T call "Tango 23, initials"

Turn early to avoid conflicting with climbing aircraft

140 Kt
1000'
Select airbrake
IN

R/T call: "Tango 23, downwind, roll/land"

THE STANDARD CIRCUIT REJOIN

speed at any stage, and this is a military equivalent of a civilian 'touch and go' manoeuvre.

■ **Threshold Speed.** This is the speed that needs to be achieved as the aircraft crosses the runway threshold, prior to round-out and touch-down. The aircraft speed must not be allowed to fall below the threshold speed figure before this point.

Torque Effects on the Take-Off Roll

Simple laws of physics dictate that every action will produce an equal and opposite reaction. Seen from the cockpit, the propeller will be seen to rotate clockwise, creating a reaction that will encourage the aircraft to roll anti-clockwise. A down-force is created on the port tyre, increasing its rolling resistance on the runway, and compounds the previously-described slipstream effect, increasing the swing to the left. On most take-off runs, right rudder will be required to keep the aircraft straight on the runway.

EGT and Torque Limits

The Tucano will be either EGT limited or torque limited, depending on ambient temperatures. The maximum permitted EGT of 650 degrees will be reached before 100% torque on warm days, and built-in sensors will adjust the fuel flow so as to maintain the maximum temperature. Consequently 100% torque cannot be achieved on hot summer days, and a longer take-off run should be anticipated.

Factors Affecting Take-Off Run Length

There are many factors that will affect the length of any take-off run, the main ones being:

■ **Aircraft Weight.** The stalling speed is directly proportional to the weight, and so a heavier aircraft must accelerate to a higher speed in order to achieve sufficient speed for take-off. Increased weight also reduces the rate of acceleration, and both factors will lengthen the run.

■ **Wind Velocity.** By making a take-off directly into wind, the aircraft will reach take-off airspeed at a correspondingly lower groundspeed, as the headwind speed is effectively subtracted from the required take-off speed. However, only the direct headwind component of the wind will affect the take-off speed and, for example, a crosswind at ninety degrees to the runway will have no effect. Likewise, an aircraft taking off with a tail wind

would require a groundspeed that is faster than the required rotation speed.

■ **Runway Gradient.** A runway that slopes upwards will cause the aircraft to accelerate more slowly, creating a longer take-off run. Conversely, a downward slope will shorten the run.

■ **Runway Surface.** Snow, heavy rain, or a combination of the two, may retard the acceleration of the aircraft, and even small depths of snow and slush can prevent an aircraft from reaching the required rotation speed.

■ **Flap.** The use of MID Flap will increase aircraft lift with only a small drag penalty and enable the aircraft to take off at a lower IAS, thus reducing the take-off run.

■ **Temperature.** Increased air temperature will decrease air density, and in these conditions a longer take-off run will be required in order to reach the same take-off speed. Additionally, the increased temperature may reduce the power of the engine and so compound the problem.

Above: A 7FTS Hawk, displaying the more warlike colours of the former Tactical Weapons Units.

Right: Hard at work, the student prepares a low-level navigation map, ready for his next Hawk sortie.

Effects of Crosswinds

Crosswinds will produce a 'weathercock' effect upon the aircraft and will additionally cause it to drift sideways. When airborne, the aircraft will drift downwind and should not be allowed to sink back on to the runway, as the sideloads inflicted upon the undercarriage could cause damage.

Effect of Flap on Approach and Landing

Extended flaps will provide extra lift, thus lowering approach and landing speeds, and creating a lower nose attitude. The additional drag created will require more power in order to fly the normal glidepath.

Windshear

Strong winds blowing over uneven ground will produce windshears, a change in windspeed, which varies with height. This can cause sudden losses of airspeed and lift, creating a high sink rate. Large power increases may be required to remedy the situation, and in strong wind conditions the pilot should anticipate windshear, increasing the approach speed as a precaution. Gusty wind conditions are also associated with cumulus clouds, and may produce windshear.

Factors Affecting the Length of Landing Run

■ **Groundspeed.** The higher the groundspeed the more energy must be dissipated during the landing run. High groundspeeds are caused by flying innacurate threshold speeds, a lack of headwind component, lack of flaps, a high weight, high outside air temperatures and a high airfield elevation (creating a higher true airspeed).

■ **Braking Technique.** When landing the Tucano, the shortest landing run will be achieved by lowering the nosewheel immediately after the mainwheels make contact, applying full reverse thrust, and application of maximum brake pressure without locking the wheels. But for normal landings, reverse thrust alone is sufficient, stopping the Tucano in roughly 2,000ft of runway.

■ **Braking Efficiency.** Water or ice on the runway

Above: The front cockpit instrument panel in the Hawk T1.

Right: Martin Baker Mk10B ejection seat, fitted to the RAF Hawk fleet. (Photo: Martin Baker)

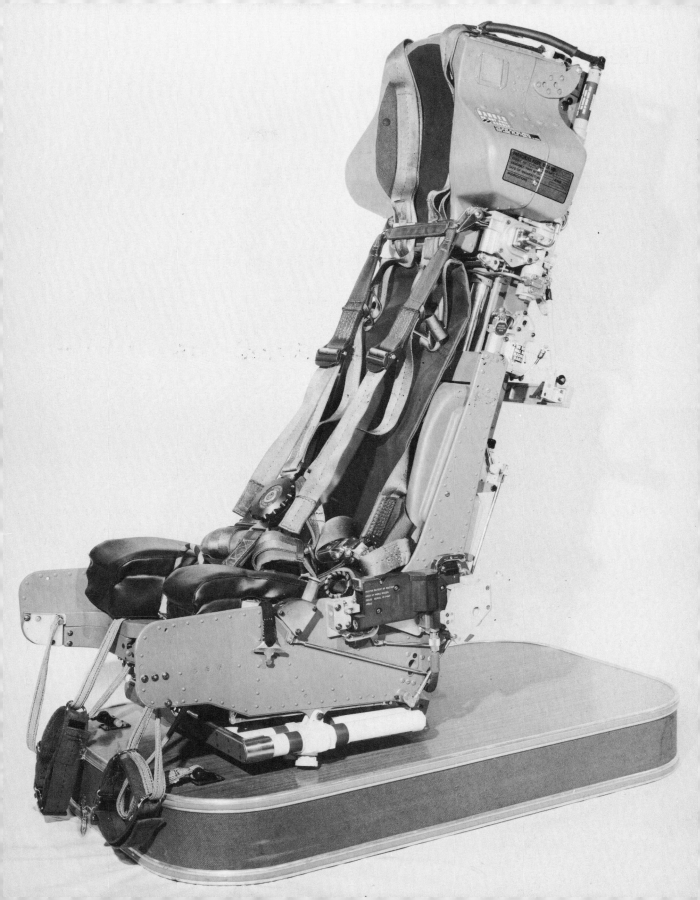

will significantly diminish wheel braking efficiency. Likewise, runways that are not treated with a 'friction course' will also reduce braking efficiency, but these factors will not alter the effect of reverse thrust.

■ **Runway Gradient.** Contrary to the affect upon take-off, a downward sloping runway will increase the length of landing run.

■ **No Reverse Thrust.** If reverse thrust cannot be applied for some reason, the landing roll will be significantly increased, by relying on wheel braking alone.

The Effect of Wind on the Circuit

Wind conditions will affect both groundspeed and track, which in turn will affect the angle of bank required in the turn on to the downwind leg. It will also affect the downwind heading, the angle of bank (AOB) and power required in the finals turn, and the amount of power required on final approach. Both crosswinds and headwinds are almost always present in the circuit, and the effects of each must be fully understood and the appropriate corrections should be made.

Wake Turbulence

A comparatively light aircraft such as the Tucano will be severely affected by the wake turbulence of even small aircraft such as the Hawk. Minimum separations, as recommended in the Flight Information Handbook, should always be observed.

Forced Landings

While it is unlikely that any student will experience any difficulties in the Tucano, the possibility of engine failure must always be considered, not least because the Tucano is a single-engine type. The Tucano glides very well, enabling students to practise forced landings regularly. However, in the event of a real engine failure the crew would always retain the option of ejecting from the aircraft, especially if far from a suitable diversion airfield. If a forced landing is attempted, and the

Left: Careful inspection of the Hawk during the pre-flight walk-round check.

pilot should fail to complete the manoeuvre successfully, the decision to eject must be taken while flying within the seat parameters. The pilot will have the clearest indication of likely success as the aircraft turns on to finals, but by this stage the aircraft will be flying with flaps and under-carriage down, causing a relatively high rate of descent. Consequently it could be fatal to eject if the height is lower than one-tenth of the rate of descent, and so the final go/no-go decision should be made at 300ft, ejecting immediately if the landing is adjudged unsuccessful.

Forces Acting in a Turn

In turns of up to 45 degrees of bank, only a slight back pressure is required on the control column, and a small amount of power, in order to maintain level flight. Almost no increase in g-force is felt by the pilot. But in turns involving a 60-degree AOB or greater, the forces increase significantly. For example, a steady 60-degree turn will register '2g' on the aircraft accelero-meter, i.e., twice the normal force of gravity. As the AOB increases, more lift is required and back pressure on the stick must be increased. But this situation cannot be sustained indefinitely, because by the time a 90-degree AOB is reached, there is no vertical lift component at all. Very steep turns also produce a large amount of drag, requiring an increase in power, which must be immediately reduced again after the turn so as to avoid accelerating.

Maximum Rate Turns

Maximum rate turns are often used in aerial combat as both an offensive and defensive manoeuvre. A tight turn will enable a fighter pilot to bring his sights to bear on an enemy aircraft, whereas a similar tight turn would allow a pilot to avoid a missile attack, if flown accurately. To achieve the best possible rate of turn, the pilot must produce the maximum amount of lift poss-ible, pointing as much of it as possible in the direction of the turn. In the Tucano the maximum

Right: A wave from the instructor as the student lines up on Valley's runway prior to take off.

The Terminology

coefficient of lift is achieved at an AOA just below the stalling angle, coinciding with the onset of light buffet. Therefore, the three requirements for a maximum rate turn are: a maximum AOB, the maximum lift coefficient (light buffet), and maximum thrust (to achieve maximum speed). Altitude also affects performance because the denser air at lower altitude will enable more thrust to be developed from the engine, and increase the amount of lift produced by the wing. However, at BFTS students are taught to achieve a maximum rate turn at a given height. Another factor to consider is the aircraft strength, and although the Tucano is stressed to withstand 7g, normal useage is limited to 6g in order to avoid inadvertent overstress or increased fatigue of the airframe. Attempting to achieve a rate of turn greater than that permitted by the 7g limit would damage or destroy the structure of the aircraft. Therefore the maximum rate in the Tucano is achieved by applying maximum power, using the maximum possible AOB, and flying at a speed which gives 5g at the onset of light buffet.

Maximum Possible Rate Turns

Despite the Tucano's reserves of power, the thrust available is still unable to balance the increase in drag during a maximum rate turn, and even at full power the speed will drop until thrust balances the drag. At about 160 knots the maximum sustained rate of turn consequently equates to about 4g at 2,000ft (roughly 130 knots and 2g at 15,000ft). As 4g is 1g less than the maximum permissible for a maximum rate turn, the deficit in thrust can be compensated by converting potential energy into kinetic energy, i.e., by descending to maintain speed. This produces the Maximum Possible Rate Turn, which can be sustained for as long as sufficient height remains.

g-Induced Loss of Consciousness

High levels of g-force will produce unpleasant effects, such as an inability to move one's head or limbs easily, and more serious effects such as blackout and loss of consciousness. Rapid increases in g can cause 'g-LOC', or g-Induced Loss

Below: The groundcrew wait for the arrival of the QFI and his student, as two Hawks get airborne in the distance.

Right: Climbing into the Hawk's rear cockpit, a QFI prepares to take his student on a low-level mission over Wales.

of Consciousness, which lasts for very brief periods, but could obviously jeapordize the safety of the aircraft and crew. If a student does experience g-LOC, he is advised to avoid repeating the manoeuvre which caused it, and to report to the Station Medical Officer after landing, to detail the circumstances of the incident. This is part of an effort to gain a greater understanding of the phenomenon. Much less serious is the gradual onset of 'greyout', a loss of peripheral vision, leading to a temporary complete loss of sight. The greyout threshold varies between different pilots, and even an individual's personal greyout threshold will vary from day to day. Naturally, if the pilot's g-limit is lower than the Tucano's, he is placing an artificial limitation on the aircraft's performance, so every student is encouraged to keep his g-threshold as high as possible. g-tolerance increases with experience, but tolerance can be decreased by other factors such as illness, lack of physical fitness, hunger, lack of oxygen, fatigue or a hangover. g-tolerance can be temporarily increased by tensing one's leg and stomach muscles during application of 'g', and by grunting, hence the sometimes rather odd noises heard on airband radios!

Spinning

One possible symptom of a fully developed stall is wing drop, which is caused by one wing stalling before the other, creating a rolling tendency towards the stalled wing. If permitted to develop further, the roll can lead into autorotation, a self-sustaining roll, with increasing yaw inputs, created by the differential in drag between the stalled and unstalled wing. If this goes unchecked, a full spin will develop, in which the aircraft, still stalled, enters a descending spiral, while rolling, pitching and yawing, behaving in a similar fashion to a gyroscope through all three axes. The Tucano's propeller compounds the problem by creating a slipstream with torque and gyroscoping effects of its own. Consequently the

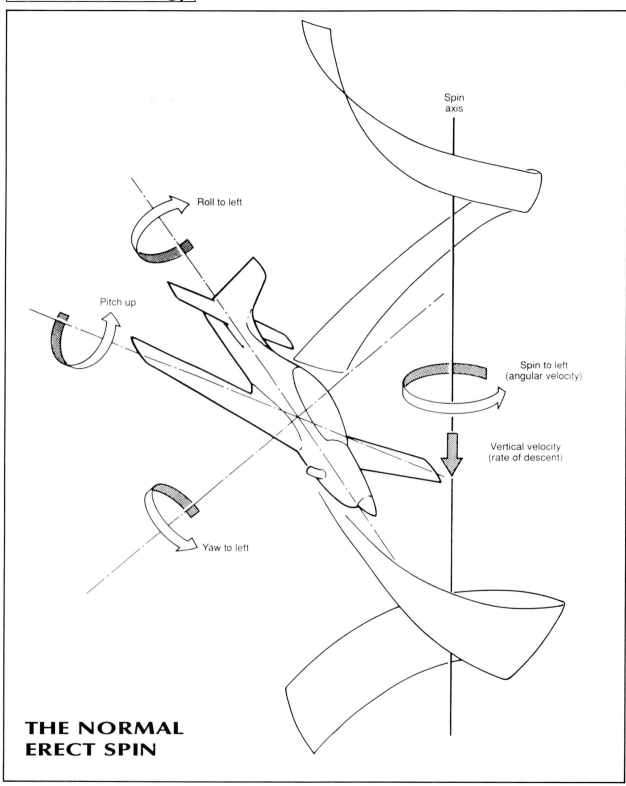

Spin axis

Roll to left

Pitch up

Spin to left (angular velocity)

Vertical velocity (rate of descent)

Yaw to left

THE NORMAL ERECT SPIN

throttle should be set at FLT IDLE during full and incipient spin recoveries.

The Terminology

The Inverted Spin

Should the aircraft be mishandled at high negative angles of attack, the Tucano could enter an inverted spin. The direction of a spin is defined by the direction of yaw, the roll and yaw direction being the same in a normal erect spin. However, in an inverted spin the directions of yaw and roll are in opposition to each other, producing a very confusing visual image for the pilot. Prolonged spinning, either erect or inverted, can cause disorientation, a reduction in the pilot's g-threshold, and even airsickness. Spinning is never practised over the sea, as the featureless surface would make visual recognition of rotation very difficult, and likewise, visibility has to be good both at entry and recovery height.

Recovery from the Spin

To recover from an incipient spin, the throttle should be set to FLT IDLE, the controls centralized, and when the rotation stops, the wings levelled. If recovery does not take place within three seconds of centralizing the controls, a full spin recovery should be initiated, as follows: check height, set throttle to FLT IDLE, check direction of turn needle, apply full rudder opposite to turn needle indication, centralize control column, and when the rotation stops, centralize the rudder. Finally, the wings are levelled and the aircraft is pulled out of the dive.

Aerobatics

Aerobatics are an important aspect of military flying, teaching student how to handle the aircraft instinctively and fluently, so that the aircraft can be used to its full potential. Aerobatics often involve large changes of speed, attitude and height, and sometimes require correspondingly large or rapid control inputs. It is important to understand how aileron and rudder inputs can have further effects than those already explored, if either or both are applied for long periods of time.

■ **Aileron.** An aircraft flying straight and level, being banked by using the aileron, will begin to sideslip towards the lower wing. Directional stability will then cause the aircraft to yaw in the direction of the slip so that while the primary effect of aileron input is roll, the secondary effect created is yaw. This effect is compounded if left unchecked, the yaw causing further roll (because the outside wing is moving faster, creating more lift, which causes even more roll), eventually developing into a spiral descent. Therefore rapid rolls require a rudder input, in the direction of roll.

■ **Rudder.** Yawing the aircraft will cause the outside wing to move faster than the inside wing, the former therefore having greater lift, which will cause a roll towards the inside wing. So while the primary effect of rudder is yaw, the secondary effect is roll. Roll rate can be increased or decreased by applying rudder.

Effect of Changing Airspeed

The effectiveness of the aircraft controls will vary depending on the airspeed, and for any given rate of response, a greater control deflection will be required at a low airspeed than for a higher airspeed. Therefore, in order to maintain a constant rate of roll or pitch when making large changes in airspeed, the deflection of the control surfaces must be varied. As speed increases, the control force necessary to achieve a given control surface deflection must also be increased. For example, during a loop manoeuvre, a light force and large deflection will be required at the top of the loop, where the speed is low, but towards the bottom of the loop a larger force and smaller deflection are necessary.

Stalling Speed During Aerobatics

Because the aircraft's acceleration changes constantly during aerobatics, so does the stalling speed, and the pilot must rely on the 'feel' of the aircraft to judge his margin above the stall. In theory, the stalling speed at zero 'g' would also be zero, whereas at the bottom of a loop, for example, where 4g or 5g may be applied, the aircraft may be close to stalling speed, and the most reliable indication is a light buffet. If the aircraft enters heavy buffet the back pressure on the control column should be relaxed, to unstall the wings. When performing aerobatics at height there is no point in taking full stall recovery action at the onset of heavy buffet, but if the aircraft should roll while in a heavy buffet the ailerons should not be used to stop the roll. The roll is an indication that the Tucano has entered an incipient spin, and so the controls should be centralized, and the throttle set to FLT IDLE, in order to recover, after which manoeuvre can be continued.

The Terminology

Effect of Torque

As previously explained, directional trim changes as power and airspeed change, and because aerobatic manoeuvres involve variations in both inputs, the rudder will be required in order to keep the aircraft in balance. Flying out of balance will allow the aircraft to wander off line.

Effect of Altitude

Indicated Air Speed (IAS) and True Air Speed (TAS are naturally the same at sea level, but the IAS/TAS ratio increases in proportion to height, until at 40,000ft TAS is double the IAS. At the same time, the force required to produce any given change of flight path will vary with TAS, whereas the amount of force that can be produced (the lift) varies with IAS. The result is effectively a reduced rate of turn or pitch, and an increased radius of turn, for any given altitude and g-loading, as altitude increases. At altitude, the decreased air density will reduce the air mass flow through the engine, causing a reduction in available torque. This will limit the amount of IAS available, in turn restricting the amount of lift that can be produced. As most manoeuvres will rely on an increase in lift, manoeuvrability is further reduced.

Mishandling

During the early attempts at aerobatic flying, the student is likely to mishandle the aircraft, sometimes temporarily losing control, and naturally it is important to take the correct recovery action quickly, in order to regain control and avoid height loss. The more likely mishandling situations are:

■ **g-Stall.** Caused by pulling back too severely on the control column at any speed. As soon as buffeting is felt, the stick back pressure should be relaxed, gently re-applying pressure after the wings have unstalled.

■ **Incipient Spin.** Ignoring buffeting and continuing to maintain a heavy back pressure on the stick will lead to autorotation, and at this stage it is important to centralize the controls and set the throttle to FLT IDLE.

■ **Vertical Recovery.** Control can sometimes be lost in or near a vertical climb, often as a result of entering a loop or vertical manoeuvre too slowly. With a low airspeed recovery cannot be immediately achieved and the pilot should try to push or pull the aircraft from absolute vertical. Throttle is set to FLT IDLE and the controls are centralized until the nose drops below the horizon. A firm grip on the controls is necessary, to counter the high 'snatch' loads sometimes encountered as the aircraft falls through the vertical plane.

■ **Inverted Recovery.** If the aircraft is in an inverted position with the nose low, the natural reaction is to pull back on the control column to recover, but this would cause a large height loss. The correct recovery is to roll erect and then pitch to straight and level as quickly as the IAS will allow.

Visual Navigation

If a line is drawn on a map, linking point 'A' with point 'B', and a protractor is used to measure the precise heading, and the time taken to get there is calculated, it would be possible, on a calm day, to go from point 'A' to point 'B' exactly on time, precisely along the line as drawn on the map. There would be no need to look at the ground during the flight. If point 'B' were not reached on this theoretical flight, there could only be four reasons why: the planning was incorrect, the aircraft was blown off course by wind, the compass in the aircraft was faulty, or the pilot didn't fly accurately. In practice, the failure to stick on track is usually caused by instrument inaccuracy or sloppy planning, but inaccurate flying and the wind factor will always produce navigational errors on every flight.

■ **Planning.** Time invested in map preparation and sortie planning is invariably repaid by confidence in the air. If the student knows that the headings drawn on the map are precise, and knows that the timing marks are correct to within five seconds, he is much more likely to adhere to the intended route, even if he is temporarily unsure of his position. Rushed planning will result in a corresponding lack of precision being carried into the air, and when things start to go wrong the first instrument to mistrust is the map; from that point on the sortie is almost guaranteed to fail. Each student is responsible for allocating sufficient time to plan each sortie, so there is no excuse for bad planning.

■ **Wind.** There is hardly ever a completely windless day, therefore it would be foolish to follow the still-air heading on the map without expecting to deviate from the path. Even a relatively light 10 knots wind abeam the aircraft is sufficient to position the aircraft two miles off

Right: Students posted to Tornado GR1 squadrons will leave either Valley or Chivenor and join the TTTE (TriNational Tornado Training Establishment) at RAF Cottesmore. From here they will join the Tornado Weapons Conversion Unit where they will learn to operate the Tornado as a weapons platform, before joining an operational squadron.

track after flying a 60-mile leg at 240 knots. In practice there is no such thing as an ideal, windless day. Before flying, the forecast wind for the chosen sortie altitude should be checked, and the following simple rules will provide an approximate drift-corrected heading and ground speed for each leg: 1. First calculate the maximum drift by dividing the wind speed by the TAS, in miles per minute (which will normally be four miles per minute). A 20-knot wind will, therefore, produce a maximum drift of five degrees. 2. Component of maximum drift should be calculated by using the clock-code system as described previously. For example, 60 minutes represents all the drift, 45 minutes represents three-quarters, 30 minutes equals half, and so on. So a 20-knot headwind at 45 degrees to track will produce a drift of roughly four degrees. 3. The head/tail–wind component is calculated by subtracting the wind angle from 90 degrees, and then using this figure in the clock-code system to determine the proportion of wind to be used. For example, a 20-knot headwind at 45 degrees from the nose represents a headwind component of fifteen knots. So aircraft speed should be increased by 15 knots in order to maintain 240 knots groundspeed. The revised figure should be written on the map.

■ **Compass Error.** The Tucano's compass is very accurate, but it could give misleading information if it is not synchronized or is faulty. The best way

to ensure against such a possibility is to check the compass continually during the sortie.

■ **Accurate Flying.** With accurate instruments, careful planning and an accurate wind estimation, there can only be one other possible cause of an unplanned deviation from track, and that is inaccurate flying. The success of each sortie ultimately depends upon the student's accuracy of flying, and consequently most of the time in the air should be spent equally divided between looking out of the cockpit for other aircraft, and looking at the instruments to ensure that the speed, heading and height are correct. Too much time spent looking at the map will result in track deviations, as will too much time spent looking at the ground. The map should be ignored until it is needed.

■ **The Stop-Watch and the Ground.** Surprisingly, it is quite difficult to navigate by making constant reference to features on the ground. Trying to identify every feature, so that there is no doubt about the precise position of the aircraft at every moment, is a recipe for disaster. Only one misidentification of a ground feature will trigger a whole chain of misconceptions until one is completely lost. Indeed there is no point in knowing exactly where the aircraft is at all times, because the provision of a suitable number of navigational fixes is included in the planned route, and if the sortie is planned properly the

Above: Those selected for the Tornado F3 will join No 229 Operational Conversion Unit at RAF Coningsby before being posted to an operational squadron. The OCU F3s form the basis of a reserve squadron, which was formerly No 65 (illustrated). This was redesignated as No 56 Squadron in 1992.

aircraft will arrive at the prescribed place at the correct time. A stop-watch is a vital navigational tool. For example, at six minutes on the stop-watch, the aircraft will be at the corresponding six-minute mark on the map. And so, as each navigational fix approaches a glance at the stop-watch will give a time that can be matched against the map's timed track, and from this the surrounding ground features can be determined, which should be visible from the cockpit. Timing, however, is important; for example, picking up the map at one minute before the fix point means that the aircraft is still four miles away.

■ **The Event Technique.** Too many fixes mean too much time spent looking at the map, stop-watch and ground. Too few fixes means un-certainty as to whether drift and speed calcula-tions are accurate. A balance must be achieved, by using the Event Technique. During pre-flight planning, all events that will require specific actions (fixes, turning-points, fuel checks, radio calls, etc.) should be planned to be accomplished at sensible intervals along the planned track. The planned time for each event should be marked on

the map. While radio calls and fuel checks should be carried out at the time marked on the map, the fixes and turning-points must be considered at one minute before the event, when the pilot should refresh his memory as to what he should expect to see outside the aircraft. At low level the events should be separated by four or five minutes, whereas at medium level a break of six minutes between events is advisable.

Low Flying Considerations

As everyone concerned with military flying knows, modern radar systems can identify aircraft operating at any altitude other than at very low level. Therefore, in an effort to penetrate enemy defences, it is necessary to fly at extremely low altitudes. Practising to fly at 250ft AGL (Above Ground Level) is a good compromise between the conflicting requirements of peace and war. This height is sufficiently close to the ground to emphasize the problems of navigation and hand-ling in this environment, but is also high enough to avoid flight safety problems, and noise annoy-

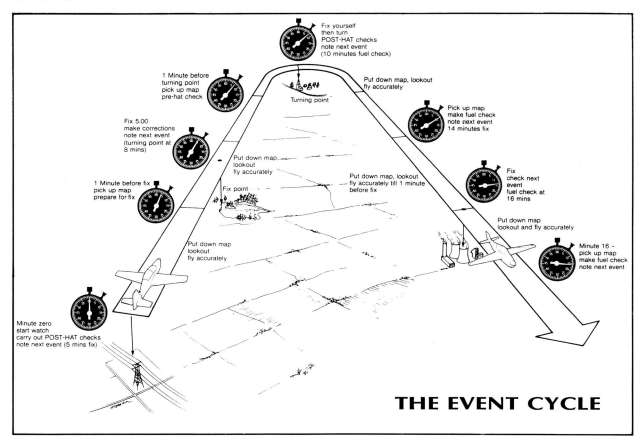

THE EVENT CYCLE

ance to the general public. Disturbing the general population unnecessarily is always to be avoided, and the following guidelines are to be observed:

■ **Never** plan to overfly towns and villages.

■ **Avoid** overflying towns and villages below 2,000ft AGL.

■ **Avoid** repeatedly flying over the same areas, during a single sortie, or series of sorties.

■ **Avoid** overflying large concentrations of live-stock, especially at sensitive times such as the lambing season.

Naturally it is not always possible strictly to observe these rules because of the high-speed environment, and from inside the aircraft it is easy to forget about the effect that the aircraft will have on the people below. The habit of minimizing disturbance is always emphasized.

Low Flying Regulations

Because the safety margins are significantly reduced at low level, many lives have been lost during the course of low flying practice. Regulations have consequently been developed that will help to protect students from making the same mistakes others have made in the past, with fatal consequences. Poor discipline at low level is considered inexcusable, and it is recognized as the swiftest way to end a student's flying career. Service aircraft are considered to be 'low flying' when at 2,000ft AGL or less in the case of all fixed-wing aircraft, or less than 500ft AGL in the case of light propeller-driven aircraft such as the Tucano, and helicopters. Low flying is prohibited unless specifically authorized, apart from during take-off and landing, being compelled to fly low due to bad weather, being directed to do so by air traffic control, or during a search and rescue duty. A pilot who has flown at a height less than 2,000ft without special authorization is expected to record the fact on an Authorization Sheet.

Turbulence

Turbulence can sometimes be severe at low level, especially when the ambient wind speed is greater than 20 knots, over hilly terrain. Instantaneous 'bumps' of up to +4g or −3g can be

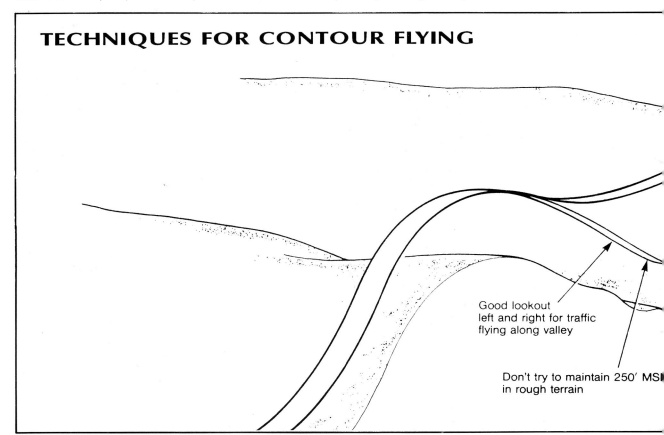

TECHNIQUES FOR CONTOUR FLYING

Good lookout
left and right for traffic
flying along valley

Don't try to maintain 250' MSL
in rough terrain

encountered, making accurate flying difficult, and even keeping a grip on the control column can be challenging. In these circumstances the aircraft should reduce speed, and climb away.

Close Formation

By the time a student reaches an operational squadron he will be able to make a rendezvous with a tanker, at night or in cloud, lead similar aircraft through instrument recoveries, and be proficient in all aspects of formation flying. Such a high standard of formation skill requires a great deal of instruction and practice, which is why a great deal of emphasis is placed on such skills throughout flying training.

Formation Positions

The two most common close formations used by front line squadrons are Echelon (for pairs recoveries and departures) and Line Astern (air-to-air refuelling). These formations will be flown extensively during flying training, both in the

Tucano and Hawk. 'VIC' is also used regularly at BFTS, as this formation enables two students to practise flying Echelon simultaneously.

Geometry of Turns

Flying in echelon requires an anticipation of the effects produced by two aircraft flying in close formation, each using a different radius of turn. For example, the wingman flying on the outside of the turn will have to climb to maintain the formation references, as the leader applies bank. Additionally, the wingman's lateral displacement results in a larger turning circle, requiring him to accelerate, and maintain a faster speed. The opposite is true for an aircraft on the inside of a turn.

Bank, Heading Changes and Closure

In straight and level flight a wingman applying one degree of bank towards his leader (and maintaining it), will produce a continuous turn and an accelerating rate of closure. Alternatively, a one degree change of heading towards the leader will produce a constant rate of closure until corrected. The concept is easy to understand, but students often fail to understand its significance. For example, if an aircraft is too wide of the leader, a small AOB should be applied to alter heading. The bank should then be taken off and opposite bank applied to turn the aircraft parallel to the leader again. Banking towards the leader and keeping the AOB applied until achieving the correct spacing will result in a very dangerous rate of closure with a significant risk of collision.

The Horizon

Formation flying requires the pilot to ignore the horizon, as the only visual references that should be obeyed are the formation data relative to the lead aircraft.

Wing Tip Vortices and Slipstream Effects

The Tucano produces a wingtip vortex which is capable of rolling a formating aircraft into the leader. It is important to maintain lateral separation between wingtips at all times. In line astern formation the effect is not a problem, but the slipstream effect will induce a pronounced pitch-up if the formating aircraft flies too high in

This aircraft can guarantee 250' MSD and will spot the potential collision risk in good time

A

Blind area to pilot B

B

Failing to anticipate sufficiently the rising ground ahead leads to 'blind' spots and the tendency to ridge clip and balloon

Where possible plan routes to follow along the 'grain' of the land

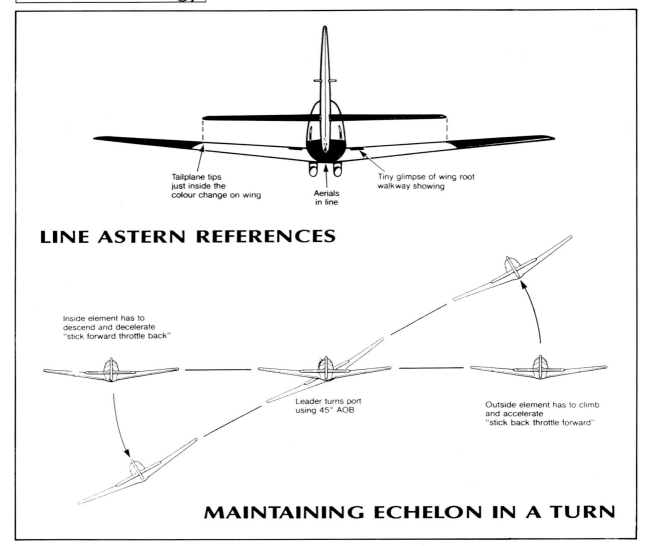

Tailplane tips
just inside the
colour change on wing

Aerials
in line

Tiny glimpse of wing root
walkway showing

LINE ASTERN REFERENCES

Inside element has to
descend and decelerate
"stick forward throttle back"

Leader turns port
using 45° AOB

Outside element has to climb
and accelerate
"stick back throttle forward"

MAINTAINING ECHELON IN A TURN

relation to the leader. The first warning sign of drifting too high is a light buffet felt through the rudder pedals.

Lost Leader in Cloud

Losing sight of the lead aircraft while in cloud is a potentially dangerous situation, as flying close to an unseen aircraft runs a high risk of collision. Likewise, the same situation could result in the student finding himself in an unusual flying attitude, in IMC, when he transfers to his instruments. Visibility problems should be anticipated, and if sight of the leader is lost the wingman must gain separation immediately, before transferring to instruments.

The procedure is:
■ Turn 20 degrees, using 20 degrees angle of bank away from the leader, and maintain the heading for 20 seconds.
■ Inform the leader of the separation.
■ If the aircraft are in a climb, continue, but if descending, level off.
■ After 20 seconds, resume the leader's original heading and proceed as instructed.

An outside wingman losing sight of the leader in a turn should roll wings level for a minimum of 20 seconds, and proceed as instructed. An inside wingman in a turn should increase bank to 45 degrees. The change of bank in all these situations is very small, and the emphasis is on immediate action rather than severe manoeuvres.

Night Flying

Contrary to popular belief, night flying is little different from flying in daylight, and in some respects it is easier, because the air tends to be smoother, and there are fewer aircraft airborne. During daytime flying the aircraft will fly with strobes and taxy lights on. At night more attention has to be devoted to their use:

■ Switch the navigation lights to BRIGHT and have the groundcrew check that all three are illuminated.

■ Leave the navigation lights on while strapping in, as an indication that the aircraft is manned.

■ Before strapping in, switch the normal interior lighting to ON and adjust the instrument and panel rheostats to give sufficient illumination.

■ Switch emergency lights to DIM and check brightness and direction of each unit before switching the system off.

■ When the chocks are to be removed, momentarily select the taxi light to TAXI, and then back to OFF. The same signal is used when ready to taxy.

■ Select the taxi light to AUTO when clearing the ASP, and with the nose pointing away from the groundcrew.

■ When well away from the ASP, adjust the brightness of the cockpit lightning.

■ The strobe lights should be selected ON, just prior to increasing power to 50% on the runway.

■ On approach, confirm that the taxi light is selected at AUTO. Landing lights are not essential.

■ Before entering the ASP, check that strobes, landing lights and taxi lights are all off.

Night Vision

Human eyesight takes roughly 30 minutes to adjust fully to night conditions, although the reverse process takes just one second. No special precautions are needed to achieve full night vision, but the pilot should preserve whatever night acclimatization he does have by avoiding looking at bright light sources such as the ASP lighting or groundcrew torches.

Night Flying Limitations

At the BFTS stage in a student's career, night flying exercises are restricted to those considered directly relevant to the learning process, and the following manoeuvres are not permissible at night.

■ Aerobatics (any manoeuvre using more than 90 degrees angle of bank or pitch).

■ Practice Forced Landings.

■ Glide circuits.

■ Run-in and break over the airfield.

■ Low flying (less than 2,000ft).

Right: To boldly go . . . Who said QFIs don't have a sense of humour?

The Aircraft

AERITALIA (FIAT) G.91T

Country of origin: Italy
Engine: One 5,000lb Bristol Siddeley (FIAT built)
  Orpheus 303 turbojet.
Dimensions: span 28ft 1in; length 33ft 9.5in; height 13ft
  1.5in.
Weight: empty 6,834lb, max 12,125lb.
Performance: max speed 586kt; ceiling 42,979ft; radius
  199 miles.
Operating countries: Italy (70+), Portugal (9).
(Specification for G.91R/1)

FIAT'S diminutive G.91 was developed in direct response to a NATO requirement for a light fighter and tactical support aircraft, issued early in 1954. A number of proposals were submitted for the design and manufacture of the aircraft, and FIAT's G.91 was selected, following the evaluation of prototype aircraft during 1957 at Bretigny in France. The first flight by a G.91 was made on 9 August 1956.

The 'Gina' (as the aircraft was affectionately called by its pilots), demonstrated an excellent ability to operate from grass or semi-prepared air strips, and a capability of carrying a variety of external stores, such as rockets, bombs, tactical nuclear stores, and air-to-air missiles, in addition to the internal Colt-Browning 12.7mm machine-guns. The first major variant of the aircraft to be built was the G.91R/1, which incorporated three 70mm focal length Vinten cameras in a revised nose fairing, which gave the aircraft an effective reconnaissance capability in addition to its comprehensive weapons fit. Entering service with the Italian Air Force, examples of this variant were also evaluated by the USAF, although the aircraft never entered USAF service. Later variants included the G.91R/1A, 1B, R3, and R4, all featuring structural reinforcement and/or improved avionics.

The G.91T was a twin-seat trainer version of the basic single-seater, with a similar performance and combat capability. Although the G.91 has virtually disappeared from military service, a handful of examples remain in

Left: 3FTS Tucano.

Below: Aeritalia (Fiat)
G91T.

use by Portugal, pending the arrival of more F-16s and Alpha Jets. Likewise Italy retains some G.91Ts, used for advanced flying training. (Photo: Tim Laming)

AERMACCHI MB.326

Country of origin: Italy
Engine: One 3,410lb Rolls-Royce Viper 20 Mk540 turbojet.
Dimensions: span 35ft 7.2in; length 35ft 0in; height 12ft 2.5in.
Weight: empty 5,919lb, max 11,497lb.
Performance: max speed 468kt; ceiling 39,040ft; radius 403 miles.
Operating countries: Argentina (4), Australia (72), Ghana (9), Italy (55), South Africa (200), Tunisia (19), Zaire (15), Zambia (18).
(Specification for MB.326GB)

The prototype MB.326 took to the air for the first time on 10 December 1957, having been designed over a three-year period. It was powered initially by a surprisingly low-powered (1,750lb) Rolls-Royce Viper 8. production aircraft (with a 2,500lb thrust engine) were first delivered to the Italian Air Force during 1962. The aircraft was specifically designed as a twin-seat basic and advanced jet trainer, although Aermacchi were quick to realize the MB.326's potential as a light ground-attack

aircraft, equipping the airframe with six underwing stores hardpoints. The aircraft can carry up to 4,000lb of weaponry, including bombs, rockets, machine-gun pods or even camera pods. The MB.326 was built under licence in South Africa, by the Atlas Aircraft Corporation (as the Impala), and by Embraer in Brazil (as the AT-26 Xavante). (Photo: Giuseppe Fassari).

AERMACCHI MB.339

Country of Origin: Italy
Engine: One 4,000lb Rolls-Royce (Piaggio) Viper 632-43 turbojet.
Dimensions: span 35ft 7.6in; length 36ft 0in; height 13ft 1.1in.
Weight: empty 6,889lb, max 12,996lb.
Performance: max speed 499kt; ceiling 48,000ft; radius 368 miles.
Operating countries: Argentina (5), Dubai (12), Italy (92), Malaysia (11), Nigeria (12), Peru (13).
(Specification for MB.339A)

In an attempt to repeat the success of their excellent MB.326 design, the sales of which totalled 784 airframes, Aermacchi developed a new, second-generation jet trainer, intended to replace both the MB.326 and Fiat G.91 in Italian Air Force service. Nine different design proposals were considered by Aermacchi, under the designations MB.338 and MB.339, and although the

Above: Aermacchi MB.326.

Above: Aermacchi MB.339.

MB.338 designs promised to offer more in terms of performance and capability, one of the two MB.339 designs was developed, largely on the grounds of smaller overall expenditure. This new design retained the 4,000lb Viper engine which had been fitted to later variants of the MB.326 (notably the 'K'-model single-seat light-attack version), but was otherwise virtually a completely new design, relying on aerodynamic knowledge gained from the earlier MB.326.

In relation to the 326, the new 339 featured a strengthened wing, a raised rear cockpit, an enlarged fin, and improvements to the cockpit layout, avionics, flying controls and cabin conditioning. The first of three prototypes made its inaugural flight on 12 August 1976, the second flying almost a year later. A total of 100 aircraft was delivered to the Italian Air Force, beginning in 1979. The aircraft is used for intermediate flying and weapons training, taking students from the SF.260 to the G.91T. Fifteen aircraft were modified to MB.339PAN standard, with the addition of smoke generating systems and the deletion of the wing tip fuel tanks. These aircraft were delivered to the world-famous 'Frecce Tricolori' aerobatic team during 1982. (Photo: via Tim Laming)

AERO L-29 DELFIN

Country of origin: Czechoslovakia
Engine: One 1,962lb Motorlet M701c500 turbojet.
Dimensions: span 33ft 9.1in; length 35ft 5.6in; height 10ft 3.2in.
Weight: empty 5,027lb, max 7,804lb.
Performance: max speed 353kt; ceiling 36,092ft; range 556 miles.
Operating countries: Afghanistan (24), Bulgaria (84), Czechoslovakia (20), Hungary (24+).
(Specification for L-29)

The first flight of the XL-29 Delfin was made on 5 April 1959, powered, surprisingly, by a Bristol Siddeley Viper engine. The second prototype first flew a year later, and following a period of evaluation, the type was selected as the basic jet trainer for each member of the Warsaw Pact, apart from Poland, which opted to proceed with the development and construction of their own PZL-Mielec TS-11 aircraft. A staggering total of 3,600 Delfins was built, with more than 2,000 being delivered to the Soviet Air Force, receiving the Nato reporting name 'Maya'. The aircraft is a rugged and simple design, capable of operations from grass strips, and equally capable of carrying armament, in the form of two 220lb bombs, or eight air-to-surface missiles, or gun pods. Entering service in 1963, the Delfin (Dolphin) was also exported to countries outside the Warsaw Pact, including Iraq, Egypt and Uganda. Most Delfins are now being progressively withdrawn, as replacements in the form of the L-39 Albatros are delivered to most users. The L-29A was a limited production aerobatic variant, and the L-29R was a dedicated attack version which never proceeded beyond the prototype stage.

AERO L-39 ALBATROS

Country of origin: Czechoslovakia
Engine: One 3,792lb Ivchenko AI-25TL turbofan.
Dimensions: span 31ft 0.4in; length 39ft 9.6in; height
  15ft 7.8in.
Weight: empty 7,690lb, max 12,346lb.
Performance: max speed 340kt; ceiling 24,606ft; Range
  783 miles.
Operating countries: Czechoslovakia (128), Iraq (20+),
  Libya (100+), Nicaragua (4+), Commonwealth of
  Independent States (200+), Romania (30+), Syria
  (90+), Vietnam (25).
(Specification for L-39Z)

The L-39 was developed as a direct successor to the
successful, and extensively-built, L-29 Delfin. Designed
in co-operation with the (then) Soviet Union, which
anticipated adoption of the aircraft as its new basic jet
trainer, the Albatros was built around a turbofan engine,
which was used in the Yak-40 feederliner, and posessed
almost twice the power of the Delfin's turbojet. Flying
for the first time on 4 November 1988, the aircraft
entered service early in 1974. More than 1,500 aircraft
have already been built, operating all over the world,
from the freezing conditions in Russia to the sands of
Iraq.

The aircraft's construction is simple, allowing easy
repair and overhaul, and likewise the flying controls are
manual, although the flaps, undercarriage and airbrake
are operared by hydraulic control. Grass field operation
is possible thanks to the high-mounted air intakes,
which avoid foreign object ingestion problems. A built-
in auxiliary power unit also enables the aircraft to
operate independently of ground support equipment.
Although the Albatros has entered service with the
former Soviet Air Force, the aircraft has proved to be
expensive to both purchase and operate, and other
aircraft options are being considered, such as a trainer
derivative of the Su-25 'Frogfoot'.

Although designed as an advanced trainer, the aircraft
also has a limited combat capability, carrying up to
2,425lb of weapons on four underwing hardpoints.
Variants developed so far include the L-39ZO weapons
training derivative, and the L-39ZA ground-attack and
reconnaissance version. (Photo: Frank Visser)

AEROSPACE AIRTRAINER CT-4

Country of origin: New Zealand
Engine: One 210hp Teledyne Continental IO-360-H
  piston.
Dimensions: span 26ft 0in; length 23ft 2in; height 8ft
  6in.
Weight: empty 1,488lb; max 2,400lb.
Performance: max speed 155kt; ceiling 17,900ft; range
  790 miles.

Above: Aero L-39
Albatros.

Right: Aerospatiale
(Fouga) CM.170
Magister.

Operating countries: Australia (47), New Zealand (14), Thailand (24).
(Specification for CT-4)

Although the Airtrainer flew for the first time in 1972, on 23 February, the aircraft has a design pedigree which can be traced back as far as 1953, when the Royal Aero Club held a competition for a twin-seat light aircraft design. More than 100 entries were submitted, the winner being the Victa Airtourer, together with its four-seat derivative, the Aircruiser. Aero Engine Services, a New Zealand company, acquired world sales rights to the aircraft, and after later amalgamating with Air Parts (NZ) Ltd to form New Zealand Aerospace Industries (now the Pacific Aerospace Corporation), the company developed a basic military trainer, based on the Airtourer design. Most unusually, the aircraft is stressed to +6g and −3g at maximum all-up weight, and is fully aerobatic. Australia's CT-4s were retired at the end of 1992, when basic training transferred to civilian contract, and Thailand's CT-4s are being progressively replaced by Fantrainers.

AEROSPATIALE (FOUGA) CM.170 MAGISTER and CM.175 ZEPHYR

Country of origin: France
Engine: Two 1,058lb Turboméca Marboré VI turbojets.
Dimensions: span 39ft 10.3in; length 33ft 0in; height 9ft 2.2in.

Weight: empty 5,093lb, max 7,187lb.
Performance: max speed 399kt; ceiling 39,370ft; range 870 miles.
Operating countries: Algeria (20+), Bangladesh (15), Belgium (18), Cameroon (10), Eire (6), El Salvador (6), France (166+), Gabon (4), Israel (45+), Lebanon (5), Libya (12), Morocco (22), Senegambia (5).
(Specification for CM.170 Super Magister)

Some 929 Magisters were built in total, and sold to a wide variety of customers, although the French Air Force was the operator of the largest fleet. Flying for the first time on 23 July 1952, the aircraft was built in response to a French Air Ministry requirement for a twin-seat jet trainer. The basic Magister, powered by two 882lb-thrust Marboré IIA engines, was later developed into the Super Magister, equipped with a pair of 1,058lb Marboré turbojets. The aircraft flew for many years with the famous French Air Force aerobatic team, 'Patrouille de France', and with Belgium's 'Diables Rouges'. While the Patrouille re-equipped with Alpha Jets, the Belgium team disbanded, although one or two Magisters still fly with the BAF in their 'Diables Rouges' colours.

Thirty-two aircraft were modified for aircraft carrier operations, and re-designated the CM.175 Zephyr, roughly half of this fleet still being in service. Like many other trainers, the Magister also has a limited ground-attack capability, and some of the CM.170's customers operated the aircraft primarily in the attack role. (Photo: Tim Laming)

The Aircraft

Left: Aerospatiale
TB-30B Epsilson.

AEROSPATIALE TB-30B EPSILON

Country of origin: France
Engine: One 300hp Lycoming AEIO-540-L1B5D piston.
Dimensions: span 25ft 11.8in; length 24ft 10.8in;
 height: 8ft 8.7in.
Weight: empty 2,055lb, max 2,756lb.
Performance: max speed 205kt; ceiling 23,000ft; radius
 680 miles.
Operating countries: France (148), Portugal (17), Togo
 (3).
(Specification for TB-30B)

Designed in response to a French Air Force requirement
for a new tandem-seat trainer to replace the Fouga
Magister, the Epsilon is based on an earlier four-seat
light aircraft, the TB-10 Tobago. The first prototype took
to the air on 22 December 1979, the second on 12 July
1980, with the first production aircraft flying in 1983,
the same year that the Epsilon entered service, with the
Centre d'Expériences Aériennes Militaires (CEAM) at
Mont de Marsan.
    Fitted with a two-minute-endurance inverted fuel
system, and stressed to +6.7g and −3.35g, the aircraft
is fully aerobatic, and the Epsilon also has a limited
weapon-carrying capability, being able to carry up to
578lb of bombs, rockets or fuel on four underwing
hardpoints. The aircraft was later fitted with a Turbo-
meca TP319 turboprop engine, and was offered to the
British Ministry of Defence as a potential replacement
for the Jet Provost, but was not selected. (Photo: Via Tim
Laming)

AEROTEC A-122 UIRAPURU T-23

Country of origin: Brazil
Engine: One 160hp Lycoming O-320-B2B piston
Dimensions: span 27ft 10.6in; length 21ft 7.8in; height
 8ft 10.3in.

Weight: empty 1,190lb, max 1,852lb.
Performance: max speed 122kt; ceiling 14,765ft; range
 497 miles.
Operating countries: Bolivia (12+), Brazil (60+),
 Paraguay (8).
(Specification for A-122)

The Uirapuru is a two-seat side-by-side basic trainer,
with a fixed tricycle undercarriage. Flying for the first
time on 2 June 1955, the aircraft was initially powered
by a 108hp Avco Lycoming O-235-C1 piston, but the
second prototype featured a 150hp Lycoming O-320-A
piston engine, which was also used in the first two pre-
production aircraft. A total of 100 aircraft was constructed for the Forca Aerea Brasileira, with a further
eighteen aircraft sold to Bolivia and Paraguay. A further
25 aircraft, designated A-122B, were constructed for the
civilian market, and were basically the same airframe,
with a revised cockpit canopy. The aircraft continues in
service, most notably with Brazil, where the aircraft is
used for primary training prior to transition to the
Tucano.

AIDC AT-TC-3 TSE TCHAN

Country of origin: Taiwan
Engine: Two 3,500lb Garrett TFE731-2-L turbofans.
Dimensions: span 34ft 3.75in; length 42ft 4in; height
 14ft 3.75in.
Weight: empty 8,500lb, max 16,500lb.
Performance: max speed 485kt; ceiling 48,000ft; range
 400+ miles.
Operating countries: Taiwan (60+).
(Specification for AT-TC-3)

Flown for the first time on 16 September 1980, the AT-
TC-3 is a twin-turbofan advanced military trainer,
designed by AIDC specifically for the Chinese National-

ist Air Force. The aircraft was developed with assistance from both the Chungshan Institute of Science and Northrop in the USA, and was based on a pair of Garrett TFE371 turbofans. Used primarily in the advanced training role, the aircraft also has a fairly extensive weapon carrying capability, and is able to fly with up to 5,000lb of external stores, in the shape of bombs, external fuel tanks, air-to-air missiles, and even aerial targets. There is provision for up to four underwing hardpoints, plus one under the fuselage, space for a semi-recessed cannon, and provision for wingtip-mounted missiles.

BEECH 33 BONANZA

Country of origin: USA
Engine: One 285hp Continental IO-520-UB piston.
Dimensions: span 33ft 6in; length 26ft 8in; height 8ft 3in.
Weight: empty 2,125lb, max 3,400lb.
Performance: max speed 181kt; ceiling 17,860ft; range 1,023 miles.
Operating countries: Haiti (2), Iran (45), Mexico (41), Spain (53).
(Specification for Beech F33A)

A hugely successful civilian design, the Beech Bonanza first flew as long ago as 22 December 1945, and the staggering production figure exceeded 15,000 examples. The first variant, the V35, featured an unusual 'butterfly' V-tail configuration, whereas the later Beech 33 and Beech 36 incorporated conventional tail surfaces. Originally called the B33 Debonair, the later C33A was fitted with a more powerful 285hp engine, and was renamed 'Bonanza', with the new designations E33 and E33A. Strengthened aerobatic versions (E33B and E33C) were later introduced, and production was finally standardized on the IO-520 engine, and the F33A basic and F33C aerobatic types.

The remaining examples in military service are all late production variants, with Spain currently the largest operator. One lesser-known variant no longer in service was the QU-22B, built for the USAF for operations in Vietnam. This was a late model Beech 36 converted for remote-control operation, and was used on seismic sensor duties under the code-name 'Pave Eagle'.

AIDC T-CH-1 CHUNG SING

Country of origin: Taiwan
Engine: One 1,450hp Avco Lycoming T53-L-701 turboprop.
Dimensions: span 40ft 0in; length 33ft 8in; height 12ft 0in.
Weight: empty 5,750lb, max 11,150lb.
Performance: max speed 320kt; ceiling 32,000ft; range 1,250 miles.
Operating countries: Taiwan (45).
(Specification for T-CH-1)

The T-CH-1 was the first indigenous design to be built by the Aero Industry Development Center (AIDC), a trainer

and light-attack aircraft based largely on the North American T-28 Trojan. The first prototype, designated XT-CH-1A, was a pure trainer variant, and flew for the first time on 23 November 1973. It was later followed by the first flight of the XT-CH-1B (with an armament capability) on 27 November 1974.

Entering service with the Chinese Nationalist Air Force in 1976, the aircraft is now Taiwan's basic trainer type, replacing the T-28 Trojan which had previously been used in this role.

BEECH 23 MUSKETEER

Country of origin: USA
Engine: One 180hp Lycoming O-360-A4K piston.
Dimensions: span 32ft 9in; length 25ft 9in; height 8ft 3in.
Weight: empty 1,494lb, max 2,450lb.
Performance: max speed 128kt; ceiling 12,600ft; range 737 miles.
Operating countries: Algeria (4), Canada (20), Mexico (20).
(Specification for CT-134A)

Flown for the first time on 23 October 1961, the Beech 23 Musketeer is a four-seat light trainer, based on the Beech 23 civilian model, of which more than 4,500 were built. Mexico took delivery of twenty airframes in 1971, for use as instrument flying trainers, equipped with screening and blind flying equipment. The second customer was Canada, ordering a fleet of twenty aircraft which were given the Canadian designation CT-134, and were used for primary flying training. These aircraft were later replaced by a new fleet of twenty CT-134A Musketeer IIs, which incorporated a more powerful engine, and these aircraft, along with Mexico's, remain in service. Algeria maintains a small fleet of BR24R Sierras, and Hong Kong was an operator of the type.

BEECH 45/T-34 MENTOR

Country of origin: USA
Engine: One 715hp Pratt & Whitney Canada PT6A-25 turboprop.
Dimensions: span 33ft 3.9in, length 28ft 8.5in, height 9ft 7in.
Weight: empty 2,960lb, max 4,300lb.
Performance: max speed 214kt; ceiling 30,000ft; range 814 miles.
Operating countries: Algeria (20+), Argentina (30), Colombia (21), Dominican Republic (10), Ecuador (17), El Salvador (3), Gabon (3), Indonesia (24), Morocco (12), Peru (6), Philippines (12), Taiwan (43), Turkey (12), USA (351), Uruguay (26), Venezuela (12).
(Specification for T-34C)

The Beech T-34 is a hugely successful basic trainer, derived from the Beech Model 45 which first flew on 2 December 1948 and was based on the earlier Model 35 Bonanza. The USAF purchased three examples for evaluation, later ordering 450 aircraft designated T-34A

Mentor. The US Navy later adopted the aircraft too, under the designation T-34B, purchasing 423 aircraft. Enjoying sales all over the world, this piston engined variant was later developed into the turboprop powered YT-34C, which first flew on 21 September 1973. This aircraft continues in widespread service, most notably with the US Navy, as its primary trainer type. The Mentor was also given a limited light-attack capability, with provision for 1,200lb of stores, carried on four underwing pylons, and this capability had been used by some smaller nations who utilize the Mentor as a forward air control and counter insurgency aircraft.

BRITISH AEROSPACE (SCOTTISH AVIATION) BULLDOG

Country of origin: UK
Engine: One 200hp Avco Lycoming IO-360-A1 B6 piston.
Dimensions: span 33ft 0in; length 23ft 3in; height 7ft 5.75in.
Weight: empty 1,430lb, max 2,350lb.
Performance: max speed 130kt; ceiling 16,000ft; range 621 miles.
Operating Countries: Ghana (10), Jordan (20), Kenya (12), Lebanon (5), Malaysia (11), Nigeria (25), Sweden (66), UK (117).
(Specification for Bulldog 120)

The Bulldog is a development of the civilian Beagle Pup, the latter flying the first time on 19 May 1969. Scottish Aviation designed and built the Bulldog, this variant making its first flight on 14 February 1971, later entering service with the Royal Air Force, where it continues in service as the RAF's primary trainer. Sweden was another major customer for the type, for use as both a trainer (with limited weapon training capability) and an Army liaison aircraft, designated as the SK61. Sweden continues to operate the type. As mentioned, the Bulldog has provision for the carriage of up to 640lb of weapons, carried on four underwing pylons. It is also capable of carrying wingtip-mounted missiles. Only one later Bulldog derivative was built, this being the prototype Bulldog 200, also known as the Bullfinch, which first flew in 1976. This was basically a retractable undercarriage version of the standard design, and although the maximum speed was increased to 150kt, the type was not put into production, and the prototype continues to fly in civilian hands. (Photo: Tim Laming)

BRITISH AEROSPACE HAWK

Country of origin: UK
Engine: One 5,700lb Rolls-Royce/Turboméca Adour 861 turbofan.
Dimensions: span 30ft 9.7in; length 38ft 11in; height 13ft 1in.

Above: British Aerospace (Scottish Aviation) Bulldog.

Above: British
Aerospace (Hawker)
Hunter.

Weight: empty 8,015lb, max 18,890lb.
Performance: max speed 560kt; ceiling 50,000ft;
  combat radius 620 miles.
Operating countries: Finland (52), Indonesia (16), Kenya
  (12), Saudi Arabia (30), United Arab Emirates (28+),
  UK (162), USA (302), Zimbabwe (7).
(Specification for Hawk Mk60)

One of the most significant military jet trainers to have
been built, the BAe (Hawker Siddeley) Hawk first flew
on 21 August 1974, entering service with the Royal Air
Force in 1976 as an advanced jet trainer, destined to
replace the Hunter and Gnat, previously used in this
role. The Hawk also replaced the Hunter in the tactical
weapons training role, being able to carry an impressive
amount of ordnance (up to 6,800lb), which includes a
30mm cannon mounted in a centreline pod, bombs,
rocket pods, air-to-air missiles, and air-to-ground missiles such as the Sea Eagle. Although regarded as being
similar to the Alpha jet, the Hawk is less expensive, is
designed to carry heavier loads, and has a longer fatigue
life. It is also a single-engined design, unlike the Alpha
Jet. The aircraft has an excellent maintenance record
(the requirement for maintenance per flight hour being
the lowest for any jet aircraft), and an equally impressive
safety record, with only a few aircraft being lost to
accidents.

In RAF service the Hawk also has a wartime reserve

role, joining Tordado F3s in a mixed fighter force,
carrying Sidewinder missiles for local air defence duties.
The aircraft is also operated by the world famous 'Red
Arrows' aerobatic team. Perhaps the best indication of
the Hawk's outstanding qualities is the US Navy
decision to purchase the Hawk in a navalized version, to
replace both the T-2 Buckeye and A-4 Skyhawk. Known
as the T-45 Goshawk, this licence-built version entered
service in 1992. (Photo: Tim Laming).

BRITISH AEROSPACE (HAWKER) HUNTER

Country of origin: UK
Engine: One 7,575lb Rollys-Royce Avon 122 tubojet.
Dimensions: span 33ft 8in; length 48ft 10.6in; height:
  13ft 2in.
Weight: empty 13,450lb, max 17,500lb.
Performance: max speed 573kt; ceiling 51,000ft; range
  572 miles.
Operating countries: Chile (28), Lebanon (6), Oman
  (15), Switzerland (128), UK (45), Zimbabwe (10).
(Specification for Hunter Mk.7)

The Hunter is certainly famous across the globe as one
of the finest fighter designs ever built, and continues to
fly, although in small numbers, both as a fighter and
ground-attack aircraft, and as a trainer. Entering RAF
service in 1958, the Hunter T7 is a two-seat trainer

derivative of the single-seat F4, retaining the combat capability of the latter variant, being able to carry bombs, rockets, external fuel tanks, as well as an internal 30mm Aden cannon.

In RAF service the Hunter continues to be operated as a systems trainer for the Buccaneer fleet, a small number of Hunters having been fitted with Buccaneer-style instrument panels, there being no twin-stick derivative of the Buccaneer. In this configuration the Hunter is destined to remain in service until the end of 1993, when the Buccaneer is retired. The Royal Navy also operates a sizeable fleet of Hunters for a variety of training purposes. Likewise, the Royal Aerospace Establishment retains a few aircraft for various trials. The largest operator of the Hunter is Switzerland, where the aircraft is still operated in its primary role as a ground-attack aircraft. (Photo: Tim Laming)

BRITISH AEROSPACE (HUNTING) JET PROVOST

Country of origin: UK
Engine: One 2,500lb Rolls-Royce Viper 202 turbojet.
Dimensions: span 35ft 4in; length 33ft 7.5in; height 10ft 2in.
Weight: empty 4,888lb, max 9,200lb.
Performance: max speed 382kt; ceiling 36,700ft; range 900 miles.
Operating countries: UK (1).
(Specification for Jet Provost T5)

The venerable Jet Provost was, for many years, the Royal Air Force's basic jet trainer, having been responsible for the sucessful training of thousands of RAF combat pilots. First flown on 26 June 1954, the Jet Provost T1 was a direct jet-powered development of the Hunting Percival

Provost piston-engined trainer. Although a small number of Mk.1 and Mk.2 aircraft were built, the standard RAF version was the Mk.3, with 201 aircraft being delivered to the RAF's Flying Training Schools. The final derivative was the Mk.5, a pressurized version, with a better fuel capacity, and a more powerful engine, first fitted in the Mk.4. The Jet Provost was exported to a variety of countries, not least in the light-attack version known as the Strikemaster. However, all have now been withdrawn from use, and just a handful of examples remain in RAF service, now that deliveries of the Shorts Tucano have replaced the aircraft. The last remaining Jet Provost is almost certain to be the Empire Test Pilots School's single Mk.5. However, the 'JP' is likely to continue flying with various civilian operators, on the 'warbird' scene. (Photo: Tim Laming)

CANADAIR CL-41 TUTOR

Country of origin: Canada
Engine: One 2,950lb General Electric (Orenda) J85-J4 turbojet.
Dimensions: span 36ft 6in; length 32ft 0in; height 9ft 1in.
Weight: empty 4,895lb, max 7,787lb.
Peformance: max speed 430kt; ceiling 43,000ft; range 621 miles.
Operating countries: Canada (114).
(Specification for CL-41)

The Canadair Tutor first flew on 13 January 1960, and was the first aircraft to be designed by Canadair (also marking Pratt & Whitney Canada's entry into the jet turbine market). A total of 160 aircraft was manu-

Below: British Aerospace (Hunting) Jet Provost.

Right: Canadair CL-41 Tutor.

Below right: Casa C-101 Aviojet:

factured, and were first delivered to the Canadian Air Force in 1963. A further twenty aircraft were built for Malaysia, and these aircraft featured an uprated engine, plus provision for six underwing weapons hardpoints. These were designated CL-41G-5 Tebuan; they have now been retired. The Tutor continues to fly with the Canadian Armed Forces as a basic jet trainer, and also equips Canada's national aerobatic team the 'Snow-birds'. (Photo: Tim Laming)

CASA C-101 AVIOJET

Country of origin: Spain
Engine: One 4,300lb Garrett TFE731-5-1J turbofan.

Dimensions: span 34ft 9.3in; length 41ft 0.1in; height 13ft 11.3in.
Weight: empty 7,666lb, max 13,889lb.
Performance: max speed 415kt; ceiling 42,000ft; combat radius 230 miles.
Operating countries: Chile (20), Honduras (4), Jordan (14), Spain (84).
(Specification for C-101CC)

The CASA Aviojet first flew on 27 June 1977, designed and built in co-operation with MBB in Germany and Northrop in the USA. The first production version was the C-101EB, known as the E.25 Mirlo in Spanish service. The next variant was the C-101BB, built for

export with a weapons-carrying capability in the shape of four DEFA 30mm guns, or two 12.7mm M3 guns, plus six wing pylons to carry bombs or rocket pods, external fuel, etc. The C-101CC features an uprated engine of 4,700lb thrust, and a greater weapons load. The C-101DD is an advanced trainer version. The aircraft has enjoyed a small export success, to Jordan and Honduras, and was licence-built in Chile by ENAER, being redesignated T-36 Halcon. The CASA C-101 Aviojet currently equips Spain's national aerobatic team, 'Patrulla Aerobatica Aguila'. (Photo: Kai Anders)

CESSNA MODEL 150

Country of origin: USA
Engine: One 100hp Continental O-200-A piston.
Dimensions: span 32ft 8.5in; length 23ft 11in; height 8ft 6in.
Weight: empty 1,000lb, max 1,600lb.
Performance: max speed 109kt; ceiling 14,000ft; range 391 miles.
Operating countries: Botswana (2), Ecuador (6), Gabon (2), Liberia (3), Paraguay (2), Peru (4), Somalia (2), Sri Lanka (6), Zaire (12).
(Specification for Cessna 150)

The Cessna 150 was, for almost twenty years, the 'standard' civilian light aircraft, sold in phenomenal numbers (23, 836), all over the world. Replaced in 1977 by the slightly more powerful Cessna 152 (of which more than 7,000 were built), the little Cessna has enjoyed a variety of sales to many countries, albeit in small numbers. There are two basic versions of the 150 and 152, one being a liaison and training model, and the other a fully aerobatic version, with a strengthened airframe, capable of withstanding +6g and −3g.

CESSNA MODEL 172

Country of origin: USA
Engine: One 150hp Avco Lycoming O-320-E2D piston.
Dimensions: span 35ft 10in; length 26ft 11in; height 8ft 9.5in.
Weight: empty 1,230lb, max 2,300lb.
Performance: max speed 121kt; ceiling 13,100ft; range 615 miles.
Operating countries: Bolivia (9), Chile (8), Colombia (30), Dominican Republic (10), Ecuador (14), Eire (7), El Salvador (7), Greece (19), Guatemala (8), Honduras (5), Indonesia (12), Liberia (3), Madagascar (4), Nicaragua (5), Pakistan (4), Panama (1), Peru (14), Philippines (12), Saudi Arabia (13), Thailand (6), Turkey (20), USA (255+), Uruguay (6).
(Specification for T-41A)

More than 36,000 Cessna 172s have been sold world wide, the largest sales figure for any aircraft at any time. Not surprisingly this inexpensive civilian light aircraft has also been sold to a large number of military air arms

as a primary trainer and liaison aircraft, but the military sales have been very small compared with those to the civilian market.

The largest military operator is the United States, which purchased 204 T-41A Mescalero as a basic trainer for the USAF, and a further T-41C models (with fixed-pitch propellers) for the Air Force Academy. The US Army also took delivery of 255 T-41Bs, of which roughly 100 remain in use.

CESSNA T-37

Country of origin: USA
Engine: Two 1,025lb Teledyne CAE J69-T-25 turbojets.
Dimensions: span 33ft 9.3in; length 28ft 3in; height 9ft 2.3in.
Weight: empty 3,870lb; maximum 6,600lb.
Performance: max speed 370kt; ceiling 39,200ft; range 870 miles.
Operating countries: Chile (20), Colombia (8), Greece (31), Pakistan (50+), Portugal (23), Thailand (15+), Turkey (65+), USA (600+).
(Specification for T-37B)

First flown on 12 October 1954, the Cessna Model 318 entered USAF service as a primary trainer in 1957, powered by a pair of Turboméca Marboré engines, licence-built by Continental (Teledyne). The first batch of 537 T-37As, with 920lb thrust engines, were later upgraded to T-37B standard, together with a batch of new-build aircraft. The aircraft was also developed to become the A-37 Dragonfly light-attack aircraft, which enjoyed good export sales around the world. Portugal's national aerobatic team 'Assas de Portugal' currently operates the T-37, and the type is also used by other Nato countries, including Germany, which owns 47 aircraft, although they are part of the USAF's Air Training Command, German pilots being trained in the USA. The USAF maintains a fleet of about 600 aircraft, although recent defence cuts will mean a reduction in numbers. A replacement design for the USAF has been under consideration for some time, but no firm order has yet been placed. (Photo: Rembert Vornholz)

DASSAULT-BREGUET/DORNIER ALPHA JET

Country of origin: France and Germany.
Engine: Two 2,976lb SNECMA/Turboméca Larzac 04-C6 turbofans.
Dimensions: span 29ft 10.75in; length 40ft 3.9in; height 13ft 9in.
Weight: empty 7,374lb, max 11,023lb.
Performance: max speed 539kt; ceiling 48,000ft; range 335 miles.
Operating countries: Belgium (31), Cameroun (5), Egypt (29), France (160), Ivory Coast (10), Morocco (24), Nigeria (22), Qatar (6), Togo (5).
(Specification for Alpha Jet E)

Right: Cessna T-37B.

Right: Dassault-Breguet/Dornier Alpha Jet.

The Aircraft

The prototype Alpha Jet took to the air for the first time on 26 October 1973, the product of a joint French and German design programme to build an advanced trainer and light-attack aircraft. Dassault Breguet of France and Dornier of West Germany each produced the type, the former company specializing initially in the trainer version, and the latter in the attack variant. Export versions have been sold to several countries, albeit in small numbers. The French Air Force is the largest operator of the type, and the Alpha Jet currently equips the famous 'Patrouille de France' aerobatic team, having replaced the Fouga Magister previously used. While Germany is disposing of almost its entire fleet (which will be sold to Portugal), the French airframes seen destined for a long career in the advanced training role. Despite the fact that the Alpha Jet is a direct competitor to the British BAe Hawk, the former aircraft has not enjoyed particularly large export sales. (Photo: Christian Gerard)

DE HAVILLAND CANADA DHC-1 CHIPMUNK

Country of origin: Canada
Engine: One 145hp de Havilland Gipsy Major 8 piston.
Dimensions: span 34ft 4in; length 25ft 5in; height 7ft 0in.

Weight: empty 1,425lb, max 2,014lb.
Performance: max speed 120kt; ceiling 15,800ft; range 280 miles.
Operating countries: Sri Lanka (5), Thailand (9), UK (62).
(Specification for Chipmunk T10)

The faithful 'Chippie' continues to fly with the Royal Air Force in comparatively large numbers, equipping both the Elementary Flying Training School (EFTS), and the Air Experience Flights (AEFs) scattered around the country. First flown on 22 May 1946, the Chipmunk was originally designed by de Havilland Canada to a Canadian Air Force requirement for a primary trainer. Following the issue of a similar British requirement, Chipmunks were delivered to the RAF, and more than 700 examples served the RAF for many years, prior to the introduction of the Bulldog, which now undertakes many of the Chipmunk's former duties. Small numbers still fly with Thailand and Sri Lanka, but the RAF looks set to be the final operator, with no replacement design having yet been identified. (Photo: Via Tim Laming)

EMBRAER T-25 UNIVERSAL

Country of origin: Brazil
Engine: One 300hp Lycoming IO-540-K1D5 piston.

Below: De Havilland Canada DHC-1 Chipmunk.

Dimensions: span 36ft 1in; length 28ft 2.5in; height 9ft 9.75in.

Weight: empty 2,535lb, max 3,748lb.

Performance: max speed 160kt; ceiling 16,400ft; range 932 miles.

Operating countries: Brazil (120+).

(Specification for T-25A)

Designed as a replacement for the T-6 Texan and Fokker S.11/12, the Neiva IPD-6201 Universal flew for the first time on 29 April 1966. Production began in 1971, with Nevia being taken over by Embraer in 1980. A small number served with Chile and, later, Paraguay, but Brazil is the only remaining operator of the type, where the T-25 is used as a basic trainer, and for weapons training, being capable of carrying a small amount of armament, including two 0.3in machine-guns, on underwing pylons. The aircraft is gradually being replaced by the Embraer Tucano.

EMBRAER EMB-312 TUCANO

Country of origin: Brazil

Engine: One 1100hp Garrett TPE331-12B turboprop.

Dimensions: span 37ft 0in; length 32ft 4in; height 11ft 2in.

Weight: empty 4,447lb, max 7,220lb.

Performance: max speed 274kt; ceiling 34,000ft; range 940 miles.

Operating countries: Brazil (124), Egypt (54), Honduras (12), Iraq (70+), Venezuela (30), UK (130).

(Specification for Tucano T1)

The Tucano was designed primarily as a replacement for Brazil's T-37 basic trainer fleet, and flew for the first time on 16 August 1980. Now in regular service with the Brazilian Air Force, the Tucano (Toucan) also equips Brazil's national aerobatic team, the 'Escuadron de Fumaca'. However, apart from enjoying a successful career in its 'home market' the Tucano is becoming an increasingly popular export machine. The Royal Air Force is now a major operator of the type, having selected the Tucano (built under licence by Shorts) as the new basic trainer, destined to replace the entire Jet Provost fleet.

The Shorts Tucano is fitted with a more powerful engine than the standard 750hp Pratt & Whitney PT6A-25C associated with the standard EMB-312. The airframe is strengthened, the cockpit, canopy and airbrake all being modified. Additionally, the Shorts Tucano is stressed to +7g (as opposed to the standard +6g), and fatigue life is increased. The Tucano was chosen by the British Ministry of Defence against stiff competition from the Pilatus PC-9, the Firecracker, and other designs.

Below: Embraer EMB-312 Tucano.

The Aircraft

Reports suggest that the RAF preferred the PC-9, and that political considerations led to the adoption of the Tucano, but whatever the reasons, the Tucano is now in regular RAF service, and is proving to be very popular with both instructors and students. (Photo: Via Tim Laming)

ENAER T-35 PILLAN

Country of origin: Chile
Engine: One 300hp Lycoming AEIO-540-K1K5 piston.
Dimensions: span 28ft 11in; length 26ft 1.8in; height 7ft 8.1in.
Weights: empty 1,836lb, max 2,900lb.
Performance: max speed 168kt; ceiling 19,100ft; range 720 miles.
Operating countries: Chile (60), Spain (39).
(Specification for ENAER T-35B)

The T-35 is an ENAER (Empresa Nacional de Aeronautica) design, built from Piper (American) components, modified locally. First flown on 6 March 1981, the first two prototypes were followed by three further aircraft which were developed by Piper, before being delivered to ENAER in kit form. The T-35A is a basic trainer with aerobatic capability (+6g and −3g), whereas the T-35B is an instrument procedures trainer; deliveries of both variants to Chile's Air Force began in 1985. Spain also purchased the type, with the designation E.26 Tamiz, and these were assembled from ENAER parts by CASA, in Spain.

FFA (FWA) 202 BRAVO

Country of origin: Italy
Engine: One 180hp Avco Lycoming AEIO-360-B1F piston.
Dimensions: span 31ft 11.9in; length 24ft 7.3in; height 9ft 2.6in.
Weight: empty 1,543lb, max 2,315lb.
Performance: max speed 130kt; ceiling 18,000ft; range 600 miles.
Operating countries: Indonesia (40), Iraq (30+), Morocco (10), Oman (4), Uganda (6).
(Specification for AS 202/18A)

Although originally an Italian design (by SIAI Marchetti), the Bravo was developed by FFA (Flug und Fahrzeugwerke AG), formerly the Swiss Dornier company, in collaboration with SIAI Marchetti. The Bravo was constructed in Switzerland, the prototype flying for the first time on 7 March 1969. Apart from the first two aircraft, all Bravos are to the same AS 202/18A standard, with a 180hp Lycoming engine. The aircraft is fully aerobatic.

FMA IA 63 PAMPA

Country of origin: Argentina
Engine: One 3,500lb Garrett TFE731-2-2N turbofan.
Dimensions: span 31ft 9.3in; length 35ft 9.1in; height 14ft 1in.
Weight: empty 5,791lb, max 11,023lb.
Performance: max speed 442kt; ceiling 42,325ft; radius 932 miles.
Operating countries: Argentina (100).
(Specification for FMA IA 63)

The Pampa was designed by FMA in Argentina, although a great deal of the design input came from Dornier in Germany, who used experience and knowledge gained from their Alpha Jet to produce this advanced trainer, which is effectively a 'scaled-down' Alpha Jet, with one engine, and a simple airframe construction. Designed to replace Argentina's MS.760 Paris trainers, the Pampa first flew on 6 October 1984. Although the aircraft has a limited combat capability, with provision for five hardpoints and a 30mm DEFA cannon pod, export sales have yet to materialize. (Photo: Kai Anders)

FUJI T-1

Country of origin: Japan
Engine: One 4,000lb Rolls-Royce Orpheus Mk.805 turbojet.

Right: FMA IA63 Pampa.

Below: Fuji T-1.

Dimensions: span 34ft 5in; length 39ft 9.2in; height 13ft 4.6in.
Weight: empty 5,335lb, max 11,023lb.
Performance: max speed 500kt; ceiling 47,250kt; range 1,156 miles.

Operating countries: Japan (55).
(Specification for Fuji T-1A)

Designed as a replacement for the T-6 Texan, the Fuji T1F1 first flew in 1957, although the T1F2, which became the production-standard trainer, first flew on 8

January 1958. Based largely on the North American F-86 Sabre airframe, the T-1 is in many respects a similar machine to the TF-86 Sabre two-seater (which was never put into production). Having served with the Japan Air Self Defence Force for many years, replacement is imminent in the shape of the Kawasaki T-4. The T-1B is externally similar to the 'A'-model, but features a 2,646lb-thrust engine. The aircraft serves as an advanced trainer, taking pilots from the T-34 piston-engined basic trainer to the supersonic Mitsubishi T-2. (Photo: Via Tim Laming)

HELIOPOLIS GOMHOURIA

Country of origin: Egypt
Engine: One 145hp Continental O-300A piston.
Dimensions: span 34ft 9.3in; length 25ft 9in; height 6ft 8.7in.
Weight: empty 1,146lb, max 1,764lb.
Performance: max speed 121kt; ceiling 19,685ft; range 485 miles.
Operating countries: Egypt (150+).
(Specification for Gomhouria Mk.8R)

The Gomhouria (Republic) originated in Germany as the Bücker Bestmann, first flown in 1939. This successful design was produced by Zlin in Czechoslovakia, eventually being developed into the Zlin 381. The Egyptian government undertook licensed production of the type in 1950, renaming the aircraft the Heliopolis Gomhouria, which first entered service with the Egyptian Air Force in 1952. Various improvements led to the Mk.8 variant, with a revised canopy design and more powerful engine. Still in service, the aircraft will eventually be replaced by the Embraer Tucano.

HINDUSTAN AERONAUTICS HJT-16 KIRAN

Country of origin: India
Engine: One 3,400lb Rolls-Royce Orpheus Mk.701-01 turbojet.
Dimensions: span 35ft 1.5in; length 33ft 7.5in; height 11ft 11.3in.
Weight: empty 6,603lb, max 10,344lb.
Performance: max speed 380kt; ceiling 39,370ft; range 382 miles.
Operating countries: India (235+).
(Specification for Kiran Mk.II)

Flying for the first time on 4 September 1964, the Kiran (Ray of Light) was in many respects an Indian version of the British Jet Provost trainer, built for the same task of basic jet flying training. Indeed the Kiran Mk.1 was also powered by the Jet Provost's Viper 2,500lb engine. The aircraft was first delivered for service in 1968, and was followed by the Kiran Mk.1A, which featured a single

hardpoint for the carriage of light stores, for weaponry training or light-attack duties. The Kiran Mk.II is a more powerful and more manoeuvrable aircraft, with four underwing pylons and a pair of 0.3in machine-guns. The aircraft remains in use with the Indian Air Force, no export sales having been made.

HINDUSTAN AERONAUTICS HPT-32 DEEPAK

Country of origin: India
Engine: One 260hp Avco Lycoming AEIO-540-D4B5 piston.
Dimensions: span 31ft 2in; length 25ft 4in; height 9ft 5.4in.
Weight: empty 1,962lb, max 2,756lb.
Performance: max speed 142kt; ceiling 19,685ft; range 462 miles.
Operating countries: India (110).
(Specification for HPT-32)

Designed as a replacement for the elderly HT-2 trainer, the HPT-32 was designed and built by Hindustan Aeronautics, flying for the first time on 6 January 1977. Two prototypes were built, neither of which met the Indian Air Force's specifications, and it was only after a series of airframe modifications that the aircraft was accepted for production, being delivered from 1985 onwards. Built primarily as a basic trainer, the Deepak also has provision for light underwing stores which will enable the aircraft to undertake weapons training and light-attack duties as required. None have been exported.

ICA IAR-823

Country of origin: Romania
Engine: One 290hp Avco Lycoming IO-540-G1D5 piston.
Dimensions: span 32ft 9.7in; length 27ft 3.5in; height 9ft 4.6in.
Weight: empty 2,006lb, max 2,624lb.
Performance: max speed 162kt; ceiling 18,375ft; range 808 miles.
Operating countries: Romania (40).
(Specification for IAR-823)

First flown in 1973, the IAR-823 is a two-seat basic trainer, with an aerobatic capability, stressed to +6g and −3g. The production variant first flew in 1974, and 40 aircraft are currently in service with the Romanian Air Force as primary trainers. However, the majority of aircraft have been manufactured for the civilian market, being sold as light four-seaters. Although the aircraft is not used for weapons training in Romania, the IAR-823 is able to carry light ordnance on underwing pylons.

Above: Kawasaki T-4.

JODEL D.140 MOUSQUETAIRE

Country of origin: France
Engine: One 180hp Avco Lycoming O-360-A2A piston.
Dimensions: span 33ft 8.3in; length 25ft 7.9in; height 6ft 8.7in.
Weight: empty 1,367lb, max 2,645lb.
Performance: max speed 173kt; ceiling 16,400ft; range 870 miles.
Operating countries: France (30+).
(Specification for Mousquetaire IV)

The Jodel D.140 was developed from an earlier design, the D.9 Bébé (Baby), flying for the first time on 1 November 1958. Enjoying good sales within the civilian market, the Mousquetaire (Musketeer), was also adopted by the French Air Force, in two versions. The Mousquetaire IV (D.140E) serves with the Ecole d'Air at Salon, as a primary trainer. A further small number of D.140R Abeille (Bee), was also purchased, for use as glider tugs.

KAWASAKI T-4

Country of origin: Japan
Engine: Two 3,660lb Ishikawajima-Harima XF3-30 turbofans.
Dimensions: span 32ft 9.7; length 42ft 7.8in; height 16ft 4.9in.
Weight: empty 8,157lb, max 16,535lb.
Performance: max speed 451kt; ceiling 45,000ft; range 864 miles.
Operating countries: Japan (115).
(Specification for XT-4)

One of two designs (the other from Fuji) submitted as a replacement for Japan's T-33 and Fuji T-1 trainers, the Kawasaki XT-4 was selected in 1981, and the prototype took to the air for the first time on 29 July 1985. However, while the aircraft was designed by Kawasaki, this company manufactures only the forward fuselage, and assembles the aircraft for flight test. The centre fuselage and engine inlets are built by Mitsubishi, and the wings, rear fuselage and tail are made by Fuji. No export orders have been received, and few are likely, but the T-4 is likely to serve as an 'intermediate' trainer with the JASDF for many years to come. Interestingly, the aircraft does have a combat capability, being able to carry up to 500lb of bombs, gun pods, missiles, or drop tanks. (Photo: Via Tim Laming)

The Aircraft

LOCKHEED T-33

Country of origin: USA
Engine: One 5,400lb Allison J33-A-35 turbojet.
Dimensions: span 38ft 10.5in; length 37ft 9in; height 11ft 8in.
Weight: empty 8,084lb, max 14,442lb.
Performance: max speed 521kt; ceiling 48,000ft; range 1,000+ miles.
Operating countries: Bolivia (32), Canada (57), Ecuador (23), Greece (47), Guatemala (2), Japan (113), South Korea (30+), Mexico (30+), Philippines (16), Portugal (10), Turkey (75+), Uruguay (11).
(Specification for T-33A)

The most famous jet trainer ever built, the T-33 'T-Bird' has enjoyed sales all over the world, with more than 6,500 aircraft constructed. The aircraft was a direct development of the single-seat F-80 Shooting Star fighter, and having first flown forty years ago, the aircraft is still, surprisingly, in widespread service. The T-33 was, for many years, the standard basic jet trainer for both the USAF and US Navy. Likewise, the aircraft was supplied to a huge number of overseas nations under the Military Assistance Programme. The aircraft was devel-oped for use as a reconnaissance platform (RT-33), and as a light-attack aircraft (AT-33). Many aircraft were eventually converted to unmanned target drones (QT-33). The T-33 was the subject of a radical re-design during the 1980s, by an American company called 'Skyfox', which produced a new aircraft (also called Skyfox), utilizing a refurbished T-33 airframe. Apart from aerodynamic modifications, the new design featured a pair of Garrett turbofans. No buyers for the design were found; however the original 'T-Bird' variant continues to fly with the air arms of many countries, and some aircraft are almost certain to remain active until the turn of the century, emphasizing the quality of this vintage design. (Photo: Via Tim Laming)

McDONNELL DOUGLAS TA-4 SKYHAWK

Country of origin: USA
Engine: One 9,300lb Pratt & Whitney J52-P-8A turbojet.
Dimensions: span 27ft 6in; length 42ft 7.25in; height 15ft 3in.
Weight: empty 10,602lb, max 24,500lb.
Performance: max speed 573kt; ceiling 38,700ft; combat radius 340 miles.

Below: Lockheed T-33.

Operating countries: Israel (30+), Kuwait (1), Malaysia (6), New Zealand (5), Singapore (12+), USA (250+). (Specification for TA-4F)

First flown on 30 June 1965, the TA-4F was a two-seat trainer development of the successful Skyhawk design. More than 130 aircraft were ordered for the US Navy and Marine Corps. Export versions were then sold to Australia (TA-4G) and New Zealand (TA-4K). However, the variant that was built in largest quantity was the TA-4J, and the type is still in regular service with the US Navy in large numbers, pending delivery of the T-45 Goshawk. Small numbers of two-seat Skyhawks will also continue to fly with the USMC until the single- and two-seaters are retired from the USMC inventory at the end of 1992. Singapore's two-seat conversion of three single-seaters led to the unique TA-4S, which features a completely separate second cockpit, positioned behind the front seat. The separate cockpit and canopy allowed the conversion to be made with few structural modifications to the basic airframe. Although the US Navy will soon retire its Skyhawks, the type will continue in service elsewhere for a few more years, albeit in small numbers. Like its single-seat relatives, the TA-4 does

Below: McDonnell Douglas TA-4 Skyhawk.

have an impressive combat capability, and is able to carry up to 10,000lb of external stores, including bombs, rockets, external fuel, etc. (Photo: Scott Van Aken)

MIKOYAN-GUREVICH MiG-15UTI

Country of origin: USSR
Engine: One 5,004lb RD-45F turbojet.
Dimensions: span 33ft 0.9in; length 33ft 1.6in; height 12ft 1.7in.
Weight: empty 7,363lb, max 11,938lb.
Performance: max speed 548kt; ceiling 48,640ft; range 833 miles.
Operating countries: Albania (6), Algeria (15+), Angola (9), Bangladesh (2), China (100+), Congo (1), Cuba (15), Guinea-Bissau (1), Guinea Republic (2), North Korea (30+), Mali (1), Mongolia (3), Mozambique (3), Pakistan (6), Romania (12+), Somalia (2), Syria (25+), Tanzania (2), Vietnam (15), Yemen (4).
(Specification for MiG-15 UTI)

First delivered to the Soviet Air Force in 1948, the MiG-15 was one of the very first jet aircraft to be developed

for widespread military use. The aircraft was powered by a Soviet-built Rolls-Royce Nene turbojet, and more than 3,000 examples were built, some being manufactured in Poland and Czechoslovakia. The two-seat trainer version was developed from the MiG-15bis, an improved fighter variant designed in 1949. More than 5,000 examples were produced. The aircraft was also built in China, as the Shenyang JJ-5, with exports being made to a few countries. The Shenyang JJ-5 is, in fact, something of a composite design, with the MiG-15's forward fuselage, and the remaining airframe being essentially MiG-17. The engine in this variant is a Wopen WP5D turbojet, a licence-built version of the Soviet Klimov VK-1A. Despite the age of the design, the aircraft soldiers on, in small numbers, and a few are likely to re-appear on the civilian warbirds scene.

MITSUBISHI T-2

Country of origin: Japan
Engine: Two 7,350lb Rolls-Royce/Turboméca Adour
   801A turbofans.
Dimensions: span 25ft 10.2in; length 58ft 7.1in; height
   14ft 4.8in.
Weight: empty 13,904lb, max 28,219lb.
Performance: max speed 921kt; ceiling 50,000ft; range
   1,612 miles.
Operating countries: Japan (88).
(Specification for T-2)

Although fighter aircraft design processes normally mean that the two-seat trainer is usually a derivative of the single-seat combat aircraft, the reverse was the case with Japan's T-2. The Mitsubishi XT-2 first flew on 20 July 1971, and entered service in 1976 as a supersonic advanced trainer with a combat capability, able to carry up to 6,000lb of external ordnance together with a 20mm cannon. The aircraft is unique in being a trainer design with reheated engines, a facility which would have applied to the Jaguar had the latter design been developed into a trainer (as originally planned) rather than an attack aircraft. The external appearance of the aircraft reveals more than a little influence from the F-4 Phantom and Jaguar general arrangements, but the aircraft was designed and built entirely in Japan. Now serving the JASDF as an advanced trainer, the aircraft takes students from the Kawasaki T-4 to the F-4 and F-15 combat aircraft. As mentioned, the T-2 was later developed into a very capable single-seat derivative, the F-1 fighter. The Mitsubishi T-2 currently equips Japan's national aerobatic team, the 'Blue Impulse'. (Photo: Via Tim Laming)

MORANE-SAULNIER MS.760 PARIS

Country of origin: France
Engine: Two 1,058lb Turboméca Marboré VI turbojets.
Dimensions: span 33ft 3.6in; length 33ft 7.1in; height
   8ft 6.4in.
Weight: empty 4,557lb, max 8,642lb.
Performance: max speed 375kt; ceiling 39,370ft; range
   1,081 miles.
Operating countries: Argentina (25+), France (48).
(Specification for MS.760B)

The Paris was developed from the MS.755 Fleuret, which was a two-seat jet trainer design competing with the Fouga Magister for the French Air Force's basic trainer requirement (the Magister winning the competi-

Below: Mitsubishi T-2.

tion). First flown on 29 July 1954, the Paris enjoyed limited success on the civilian market as a light executive jet, and some models were sold to the military air arms of Brazil and Argentina. However, the main buyer was the French Air Force and Navy, where roughly 40 aircraft remain in service. Argentina maintains a small fleet of Paris IIs, used for weapons training and counter insurgency duties.

MUDRY CAP 10/20/21

Country of origin: France
Engine: One 180hp Avco Lycoming AEIO-360-B2F piston.
Dimensions: span 26ft 5.3in; length 23ft 5.9in; height 8ft 4.4in.
Weight: empty 1,190lb, max 1,830lb.
Performance: max speed 146kt; ceiling 16,405ft; range 746 miles.
Operating countries: France (72), Mexico (20), Morocco (9).
(Specification for CAP 10)

The Mudry CAP 10 first flew in August 1968, developed from a two-seat light aircraft produced in kit form. Stressed for aerobatics, the CAP 10 is cleared to +6g and −4.5g, and the aircraft has been sold extensively on the civilian market as a popular sports plane. The French Air Force and Navy currently utilize the aircraft as an elementary trainer, in both the original version and the CAP 10B variant, which features an enlarged vertical tail surface. Later versions include the CAP 20, a single-seat aerobatic type, and the CAP 21 with a revised wing aerofoil section, some of the latter type being purchased by the French Air Force. The Cap 10 currently equips Morocco's national aerobatic team.

NORTH AMERICAN T-6 TEXAN

Country of origin: USA
Engine: One 550hp Pratt & Whitney R-1340-AN-1 piston.
Dimensions: span 42ft 0.25in; length 29ft 6in; height 11ft 9in.
Weight: empty 4,158lb, max 5,300lb.
Performance: max speed 178kt; ceiling 21,500ft; range 750 miles.
Operating countries: Bolivia (4), Dominican Republic (2), Paraguay (12), South Africa (60+), UK (2), Uruguay (2).
(Specification for AT-6C)

The most famous trainer aircraft of all, the North American T-6 first flew well over 50 years ago, and surprisingly, the type is still serving a variety of military air arms. More than 16,000 examples were produced, and although the T-6 was designed purely as a trainer, many export aircraft were used for counter-insurgency and light attack duties, thanks to the Texan's ability to carry small bombs and a machine-gun. South Africa is currently the largest operator of the type, although replacement is now in sight. Two aircraft (designated Harvard in RAF service) continue to fly with the Aeroplane and Armament Experimental Establishment at Boscombe Down, used primarily for chase and photo-graphic work, and even when the last aircraft leave military service, the T-6 looks set to continue flying on the civilian warbirds scene, with hundreds of examples already flying in the markings of former military operators. (Photo: Via Tim Laming)

Below: North American T-6 Texan.

NORTH AMERICAN T-28 TROJAN

Country of origin: USA
Engine: One 1,425hp Wright Cyclone R-1820-86
 piston.
Dimensions: span 40ft 1in; length 33ft 0in; height 12ft
 8in.
Weight: empty 6,424lb, max 8,500lb.
Performance: max speed 298kt; ceiling 35,500ft; range
 1,060 miles.
Operating countries: Mexico (20), Philippines (20+),
 South Korea (15+), Uruguay (4).
(Specification for T-28B)

Flown for the first time on 24 September 1949, the North
American T-28 was designed as a replacement for the
T-6 Texan primary trainer, used by the USAF's Air
Training Command. More than 1,000 T-28As were built
for the USAF, many surviving in service until the end of
the fifties. The more powerful T-28B and T-28C (with a
strengthened airframe and arrester hook) were built for
the US Navy and Marine Corps, and served with
distinction until the advent of the T-34 during the
seventies. The T-28D was exported to many overseas
countries, used as a light attack counter-insurgency
aircraft, and a handful of Trojans still fly in this role.
However, the larger number of active Trojans now fly as
civilian warbirds, carrying the colourful markings once
worn by previous military operators.

NORTHROP T-38 TALON

Country of origin: USA
Engine: Two 3,850lb General Electric J85-GE-5
 turbojets.
Dimensions: span 25ft 3in; length 46ft 4.5in; height 12ft
 10.5in.
Weight: empty 7,174lb, max 11,820lb.
Performance: max speed 745kt; ceiling 53,600ft; range
 1,093 miles.
Operating countries: Portugal (12), Turkey (20), USA
 (865+).
(Specification for T-38A)

Developed in parallel with the single-seat F-5A, the
Northrop T-38 Talon began life as the N-156T, a private
venture until the USAF issued a specifcation for a jet
trainer in 1956. The Talon made its first flight on 10
April 1959, powered by a pair of General Electric YJ85-
GE-5 engines, each developing 2,100lb of thrust.
However, the first production aircraft (flown early in
1960) featured modified engines with reheat, giving
each engine an additional 1,500lb of thrust and
enabling the Talon to achieve supersonic (Mach 1.3)
flight – quite an achievement for a trainer. Having
entered USAF service in 1961, the Talon continues to be
operated by USAF Air Training Command, and with no
replacement selected as yet, the aircraft looks set for
years of continued service. Portugal and Turkey operate

Left: Northrop T-38 Talon.

small numbers of Talons, and likewise, Germany maintains a fleet of T-38s, in USAF markings, as part of their USA-based training programme. The aircraft is also used by NASA, for research and training duties. (Photo: Fritz Becker)

PILATUS PC-7 TURBO-TRAINER

Country of origin: Switzerland
Engine: One 650hp Pratt & Whitney Canada PT6A-25A turboprop.
Dimensions: span 34ft 1.4in; length 32ft 1in; height 10ft 6.4in.
Weight: empty 2,932lb, max 5,952lb.
Performance: max speed 196kt; ceiling 26,000ft; range 1,634 miles.
Operating countries: Angola (16), Austria (16), Bolivia (22), Burma (15), Chad (2), Chile (10), Guatemala (10), Iraq (30+), Malaysia (42), Mexico (85), Switzerland (39).
(Specification for PC-7)

A particularly successful design, the Pilatus PC-7 flew for the first time on 12 April 1966, as a redesigned P-3, with a turboprop engine. Initially the design created

Below: Pilatus PC-7 Turbo-Trainer.

little interest from potential buyers, and it was not until the late seventies that a much-improved version was sold to a variety of countries, including 'home deliveries' to the Swiss Air Force. The Turbo-Trainer is fully aerobatic (+6g and −3g), and capable of carrying underwing stores up to 2,293lb, a provision much appreciated by many countries which use the aircraft for weapons training and light attack duties. (Photo: Paul Hoehn)

PILATUS PC-9

Country of origin: Switzerland
Engine: One 1,150hp Pratt & Whitney Canada PT6A-62 turboprop.
Dimensions: span 33ft 2.4in; length 33ft 4.8in; height 10ft 8.3in.
Weight: empty 3,715lb, max 7,055lb.
Performance: max speed 300kt; ceiling 38,000ft; range 955 miles.
Operating countries: Australia (67), Burma (7), Saudi Arabia (30), Switzerland (4).
(Specification for PC-9)

Despite the entry into RAF service of the Shorts Tucano, many observers (including countless RAF pilots) regard

Above: Pilatus PC-9.

the PC-9 as being the aircraft that should have been purchased for the RAF, in preference to the Tucano. Certainly a comparison of the performance tables illustrates that the PC-9 does out-perform the Tucano in every respect, but of course, such a direct comparison does not account for costs, job considerations, and so on. Regardless of the rights and wrongs of the British Government's decision, it is clear that the growing number of PC-9 operators are acquiring what is probably the best multi-purpose trainer currently in production.

Despite the fact that the aircraft is a direct development of the earlier PC-7, there is only a 10 per cent commonality of parts between the two designs. The aircraft first flew on 7 May 1984, and seems set to become a very popular aircraft throughout the world, both as a trainer and as a limited combat aircraft with provision for up to 2,293lb of external ordnance. (Photo: Tim Laming)

PZL MIELEC TS-11 ISKRA

Country of origin: Poland
Engine: One 2,425lb IL SO-3W turbojet.
Dimensions: span 33ft 0in; length 36ft 7in; height 11ft 5.8in.

Weight: empty 5,655lb, max 8,466lb.
Performance: max speed 415kt; ceiling 37,730ft; range 783 miles.
Operating countries: India (38), Poland (95+).
(Specification for TS-11)

Another early sixties design, still in regular service, the Iskra (Spark) was designed and built as a potential jet trainer for the Soviet Air Force; however the type was not selected, and only Poland and India adopted the aircraft, for use as both an advanced flying and weapons trainer. The Iskra airframe is constructed to withstand the rigours of +8g and −4g, which is pretty impressive considering the age of the design. As recently as 1982 the aircraft was back in production, but both Poland and India will shortly replace the type.

PZL WARSZAWA-OKECIE PZL-130T TURBO-ORLIK

Country of origin: Poland
Engine: One 550hp Pratt & Whitney PT6A-25A turboprop.
Dimensions: span 26ft 3in; length 28ft 5.5in; height 11ft 7in.
Weight: empty 2,536lb, max 4,358lb.
Performance: max speed 256kt; ceiling 33,000ft; range

Above: Rockwell International T-2 Buckeye.

1,198 miles.
Operating countries: Poland (48).
(Specification for PZL-130T)

Based on the earlier PZL-130 (radial) piston-engined Orlik, the later turboprop derivative was developed by Airtech in Canada, where the PZL-130T prototype first flew in August 1986. Unfortunately the aircraft later crashed, but the programme went ahead, and in addition to civilian sales, the type has been adopted by the Polish Air Force.

ROCKWELL INTERNATIONAL T-2 BUCKEYE

Country of origin: USA
Engine: Two 2,950lb General Electric J85-GE-4 turbojets.
Dimensions: span 38ft 1.5in; length 38ft 3.5in; height 14ft 9.5in.
Weight: empty 8,115lb, max 13,190lb.
Performance: max speed 460kt; ceiling 45,500ft; range 1,070 miles.
Operating countries: Greece (36), USA (200+), Venezuela (20).
(Specification for T-2C)

Flying for the first time on 31 January 1958, the YT2J-1 was the first of six pre-production aircraft designed by North American Aviation, to fulfil the US Navy's requirement for an 'intermediate' trainer, taking students from the basic phase through to advanced flying. These early Buckeyes were powered by just one Westinghouse J34 engine, developing 3,400lb of thrust. The T-2A was followed by the T-2B, which first flew in August 1962, powered by two Pratt & Whitney J60s, increasing thrust to 6,000lb. The T-2C switched to General Electric J85 engines, and it is this last variant which still serves with the US Navy in relatively large numbers. Replacement is imminent, however, with the delivery of T-45 Goshawks. The Buckeye also continues to fly with both Greece and Venezuela, the latter country still utilizing the T-2's capability to carry underwing stores up to 3,500lb in weight. (Photo: Tim Laming)

SAAB 105

Country of origin: Sweden
Engine: Two 1,640lb Turboméca Aubisque turbofans.
Dimensions: span 31ft 2in; length 34ft 5.4in; height 8ft 10.3in.
Weight: empty 5,534lb, max 8,929lb.
Performance: max speed 415kt; ceiling 44,290ft; range 870 miles.
Operating countries: Austria (30), Sweden (134+).
(Specification for Sk60A)

Developed as a private venture by Saab, their Model 105 first flew on 29 June 1963, and following evaluation by the Swedish Air Force the type was purchased for use as a trainer, close air support, reconnaissance and liaison aircraft. The trainer and liaison variant is given the Swedish designation Sk60A, the light-attack version being the Sk60B, and the reconnaissance type the Sk60C. The Saab 105XT features uprated (2,850lb) engines, and a toughened airframe. Purchased by the Austrian Air Force, the aircraft remains in use, together with the Swedish fleet, with no replacement on the horizon as yet. Both the Austrian (Karo As) and Swedish (Team 60) national aerobatic teams utilize the Saab 105. (Photo: Tim Laming)

SAAB MFI-15/17

Country of origin: Sweden
Engine: One 200hp Avco Lycoming IO-360-A1B6 piston.
Dimensions: span 29ft 0.4in; length 22ft 11.6in; height 8ft 6.4in.
Weight: empty 1,424lb, max 2,646lb.
Performance: max speed 127kt; ceiling 13,450ft; range 560+ miles.
Operating countries: Denmark (29), Norway (17), Pakistan (80+), Zambia (20).
(Specification for MFI-17 Supporter)

The Saab MFI-15 first flew on 11 July 1969, and was developed into a successful civilian light aircraft used for pleasure flying and for many other activities, including highway patrol and air ambulance. Only one military buyer was found, however, this being Norway, where the MFI-15 Safari is used as a primary trainer. The aircraft was later developed into the MFI-17 Supporter, with the same engine, but with a strengthened airframe and underwing hardpoints, intended primarily for military purchase. The aircraft was sold successfully, and was built under licence in Pakistan, where the type is known as the Mushshak.

SIAI-MARCHETTI S.211

Country of origin: Italy
Engine: One 2,500lb Pratt & Whitney Canada JT15D-4C turbofan.
Dimensions: span 27ft 7.9in; length 30ft 6.5in; height 12ft 5.6in.
Weight: empty 3,627lb, max 6,834lb.
Performance: max speed 360kt; ceiling 40,025ft; range 1,036 miles.
Operating countries: Singapore (29).
(Specification for S.211)

The prototype S.211 first flew on 10 April 1981, designed as a low cost, high technology jet trainer with a light-attack capability. The aircraft is equipped to carry up to 1,455lb of external stores on four underwing hardpoints. Sales have not been particularly impressive, however, with Haiti's fleet being re-sold to a US buyer.

Above: Saab 105.

Above: Siai-Marchetti SF.260.

Singapore retains its fleet of aircraft, which were built by Singapore Aircraft Industries from SIAI-manufactured kits.

SIAI-MARCHETTI SF.260

Country of origin: Italy
Engine: One 260hp Avco Lycoming O-540-E4A5
 piston.
Dimensions: span 27ft 4.7in; length 23ft 3.5in; height
 7ft 10.9in.
Weight: empty 1,698lb, max 2,866lb.
Performance: max speed 165kt; ceiling 14,700ft; range
 173 miles.
Operating countries: Belgium (28), Bolivia (3), Brunei
 (2), Burundi (7), Eire (11), Italy (30), Libya (260+),
 Nicaragua (6), Philippines (35+), Singapore (26),
 Somalia (4), Thailand (12), Tunisia (18), United Arab
 Emirates (5), Zaire (9), Zimbabwe (30).
(Specification for SF.260 Warrior)

Aviamilano Construzioni Aeronautiche flew the prototype Aviamilano F-250 on 15 July 1954. The aircraft was constructed under licence by SIAI-Marchetti, which designated the aircraft SF.260. Civilian sales were disappointing, and the company later redeveloped the aircraft as the SF.260M, aimed at military sales. Further development led to the SF.260W Warrior, with a light offensive capability, able to carry machine-guns, gun pods, reconnaissance pods or small bombs. The aircraft has enjoyed great success on the military market, and

the SF.260 is likely to be in service for many more years. (Photo: Boudewijn Pieters)

SOCATA RALLYE

Country of origin: France
Engine: One 235hp Avco Lycoming O-540-B4B5
 piston.
Dimensions: span 31ft 11.5in; length 23ft 9.4in; height
 9ft 2.2in.
Weight: empty 1,565lb, max 2,976lb.
Performance: max speed 148kt; ceiling 14,765ft; range
 640 miles.
Operating countries: Djibouti (1), Dominican Republic
 (1), France (15), Libya (8), Morocco (2), Rwanda (2),
 Senegambia (8).
(Specification for R.235 Guerrier)

First flown on 10 June 1959, the Rallye was designed by Morane-Saulnier, which was later taken over by Potez, this company then becoming part of Sud Aviation, called SOCATA (Société de Construction d'Avions de Tourisme et d'Affaires). The latter subsidiary was devoted to the development and sales of the Rallye series. Enjoying good civilian sales, the type has also been sold in various configurations to quite a few countries for use as a trainer, liaison and counter-insurgency aircraft, with provision for air-to-surface rockets, machine-guns, practice bombs, even a surveillance pod. The Guerrier (Warrior) continues to fly in small numbers throughout the world.

The Aircraft

SOKO G-2 GALEB/G-4 SUPER GALEB

Country of origin: Yugoslavia
Engine: One 2,500lb Rolls-Royce Viper 11 Mk22-6
  turbojet.
Dimensions: span 31ft 11.1in; length 33ft 11.1in; height
  10ft 9.1in.
Weight: empty 5,776lb, max 9,480lb.
Performance: max speed 439kt; ceiling 39,370ft; range
  771 miles.
Operating countries: Libya (30+), Yugoslavia (50+),
  Zambia (8).
(Specification for G-2A Galeb)

The SOKO G-2A Galeb (Seagull) first flew in 1961,
designed as a basic jet trainer for the Yugoslav Air Force.
The export version, designated G-2A-E, enjoyed a
limited success with an updated avionics and radio fit.
The type does posess a limited attack capability, with
0.5in machine-guns and 220lb of underwing stores. The
Galeb's replacement has also been designed by SOKO,
in the shape of the G-4 Super Galeb. Although the name
is similar, the G-4 is a completely new aircraft, with a
4,000lb Rolls-Royce Viper and a maximum speed of
491kt. Structural improvements have been incorporated
as well as better avionics. Likewise the ordnance-
carrying capability has also been improved. At present,
only the Yugoslav Air Force has purchased the Super
Galeb. (Photo: Fritz Becker)

VALMET L-70

Country of origin: Finland
Engine: One 200hp Avco Lycoming AEIO-360-A1B6
  piston.
Dimensions: span 31ft 7.1in; length 24ft 7.3in; height
  10ft 10.3in.
Weight: empty 1,691lb, max 2,293lb.
Performance: max speed 127kt; ceiling 16,405ft; range
  590 miles.
Operating countries: Finland (28).
(Specification for L-70)

Designed by the Valmet Corporation in response to a
Finnish Air Force requirement for a basic trainer, the
prototype Valmet-Leko-70, first flew on 1 July 1975. The
Air Force ordered 30 examples, naming the aircraft
'Vinka', and the last airframe was delivered in 1982. The
airframe is stressed to +6g and −3g, and is fully
aerobatic. In addition to its training role, the Vinka is
used for liaison and observation duties. Sales of the type
for both the civilian and military market have been
surprisingly small. (Photo: Via Tim Laming)

Below: Valmet L-70.